In the pages of *Present* I felt the gen
out onto my back patio to listen for
blue jays. As a fellow pastor and par.... ....y ...... s nard-won
wisdom and humorous encouragement connected deeply with my
restless soul. This book will embrace the weary, the too busy, and
anyone longing to be more present in their daily lives—and point
them to the rest and presence of Jesus.

APRIL FIET, pastor and author of *The Sacred Pulse:
Holy Rhythms for Overwhelmed Souls*

I finished Courtney's book on the same day I reached the end of a
week-long project. Just when I was about to move on to my next
chore, I could almost hear Courtney telling me to pause, to be fully
present in this moment. So I surveyed my work and savored a job
well done, and in so doing, I crowned it with a mysterious "something
more" that Courtney invites you to experience for yourself in this
volume of personal stories suffused with scriptural lessons.

DR. CHRISTOPHER UPHAM, philosopher, father,
and farmer

Courtney Ellis encourages us to slow down, to look up, to look
around, and to witness the relationships and the holy ground that
surround us. Being *present in the now* and recognizing *the gift of
being all in* are difficult to do, but the author presents us with ways to
position our lives and attitudes so these things can become a reality.
Whether you are well-seasoned in your spiritual life or a novice like
most of us, Ellis's book will bring you into a deeper understanding
of the richness of living into every moment.

REV. DR. ROSS PURDY, pastor, First Presbyterian Church,
Burbank, CA

Those of us who struggle with a sense of rootlessness, discontent, and distraction will find hope in the pages of *Present*. With humility and humor, Courtney Ellis weaves the story of her own struggles together with the convictions and wisdom of her Christian faith, in order to shed light on a path that leads to growth. This book provides a hopeful and grounded alternative to the unattentive and rushed haze that so many call living.

REV. DR. JACKSON CLELLAND, pastor, Presbyterian Church of the Master, Mission Viejo, CA

● ● ●

We hear the well-meaning advice that we're supposed to bloom where we've been planted. But when our mobile culture and consumerist mindset keep us always on the move, we learn to keep our roots shallow and our connections superficial. Courtney Ellis challenges us to be all in, right where we are. *Present* is an invitation to explore what it means to show up for the abundant life God offers us, written with Ellis's trademark honesty, humor, and insight. Highly recommended!

MICHELLE VAN LOON, author of *Born to Wander: Recovering the Value of Our Pilgrim Identity*

● ● ●

This book is a great gift. Courtney Ellis helps us see the grace that surrounds us right where we are, and she invites us into the practices and postures that will permit us to partake of that grace. Since being a person means living in a particular time and place and with a particular people—and in no other time or place and with no other people—we need to heed this invitation to live the particular lives that God calls us to, and in which we will see his faithfulness.

DR. CHRIS BLUMHOFER, associate professor of New Testament, Fuller Theological Seminary

The author shares personal stories and Scripture messages to help folks understand how we can bloom where we are planted. This book is a joy to read and helpful for those of us living in the same place for many years as well as those who relocate frequently.

PASTOR CAROL P. TAYLOR, United Church of Beloit, WI

● ● ●

Sometimes God calls us to stay. With wit, insight, and a pastor's heart, Rev. Courtney Ellis helps us honor this call. By sharing how she has deepened her own connections, Courtney guides us in how we, too, can stay put well.

REV. JON SAUR, senior pastor, StoneBridge Community Church, Simi Valley, CA

● ● ●

With a posture of generosity and a writing style that is both warm and engaging, Rev. Courtney Ellis's tender care for her readers shines through in *Present*. In this book, Courtney gently invites us to return to this moment *and* to be with this moment, while honoring the nuance and complexity of what it means to be present. You will not only walk away from this book with the deep wisdom she offers, but also be further motivated to prioritize the practice of presence.

HOLLY K. OXHANDLER, PhD, LMSW, associate dean for research and faculty development at Baylor University's Diana R. Garland School of Social Work, cohost of *CXMH: A Podcast on Faith & Mental Health*, and author of *The Soul of the Helper*

In *Present*, Courtney extends an invitation that's both graceful and practical: the invitation to live lives that bless us, the people around us, and our communities with the gift of being truly rooted.

ROBERT VORE, therapist and cohost of *CXMH: A Podcast on Faith & Mental Health*

With her signature wit, storytelling, and grace, Ellis invites us off the treadmill of searching for the next big thing, daring us to take up the adventure of staying right where we are. This book is somehow a challenge and a balm, and most of all, a reminder of the grace and care of a deeply present God.

LYNDSEY MEDFORD, author of *My Body and Other Crumbling Empires: Lessons for Healing in a World That Is Sick*

Only Courtney Ellis can quote Bonhoeffer, *The Princess Bride*, and St. Anne (Lamott) while challenging us to better know and be known. Her stories are as grounded as her family's backyard garden, springing from the soil of making peace with a place. As a Midwestern transplant to California, Ellis shares perspective through geography and season, recounting tales of blizzards, whitewater, and thunderstorms alongside the joys of noticing the birds of the air and West Coast lilies of the field. The simple act of reading this book and showing up on a neighbor's front step can revolutionize the world.

BETHANY RYDMARK, landscape architect, garden designer, and writer

present

THE GIFT OF BEING ALL IN,
RIGHT WHERE YOU ARE

COURTNEY ELLIS

AspirePress

Present: The Gift of Being All In, Right Where You Are
© 2023 Courtney Ellis

Published by Aspire Press
An imprint of Tyndale House Ministries
Carol Stream, Illinois
www.hendricksonrose.com

ISBN: 978-1-6286-2895-1

Cover design: Libby Dykstra
Internal design: Cristalle Kishi

Cover image: johnwoodcock, iStock

Excerpt from "What I Wish You'd Heard" taken from *Lines from the Provinces*, by David Wright. Used with permission.

Library of Congress Control Number: 2022040250

Printed in the United States of America
010922VP

To Sonia Justl Ellis—
a present of a friend

Contents

Foreword

by Aarik Danielsen

I WASTED TIME treating some verbs as holier than others.

Attending a Christian university—where missions was elevated and every spiritual stirring encouraged—*go* seemed like the most sacred action word. A decade and a head full of Wendell Berry dreams later, *stay* piously dug in its heels.

I have been the young man who chased a calling 1,257 miles from home to college; the twenty-something who followed God around the globe yet failed to belong anywhere.

I have also planted roots, taking up a front-porch seat to watch my Midwest community change by degrees. And I have stayed long enough at the same job, the same church, the same zip code—well after so many left—to watch myself become a ghost.

We place our faith in verbs because of myths we learn to carry. In the book you are about to read, my friend Courtney Ellis gently strips such myths away with tiny but profound proverbs, and observations from the longer view. There are no greener pastures, no perfect choices. My life sounds an "amen" to Courtney's words.

Stay or go, stake or uproot—no verb is inherently holy. Our words, and the choices they represent, become virtuous only when acted on by the most proper noun there is: God, the ever-present one, in whom we live and move and have our being.

But Courtney does so much more here, demonstrating how presence is a daily practice and a sermon we must preach to ourselves—that, yes, we can find God in whatever place we're in and love particular people particularly.

Courtney is, too, good a writer—and pastor—to spell out how to achieve present-tense living, as if it were a skill easily mastered rather than an art to refine. Instead, she describes her life and the lives of others in process toward presence. She asks good questions, ones worth wrestling.

Most importantly, she acquaints us with a God whose presence is as boundless as all the oceans set side by side—yet closer than your next heartbeat. When we fix our gaze on this God, we become what we behold. He teaches us to cherish any and every corner of the world he animates and inhabits, to hold them close the way he does.

Some passages of *Present* immediately feel like freedom; others lay out limits. Keep reading. Courtney never calls us to settle, but to grow settled from the inside out. She describes a life limited by love: bound by people, places, and things, but shot through with God's promises.

Growing satisfied within his presence, we are free to stop asking too much of others, enjoying every moment and everyone—including ourselves—exactly as they are.

Mary Oliver wanted to come alive in quiet woods. Jack Kerouac hit the highways in search of mad people. Eugene Peterson favored a long obedience in the same direction. Any and all our ways of moving through the world can be holy, once we let God set the boundaries of our lives, trusting he will fill them with himself.

—Aarik Danielsen
Journalist and *Fathom Mag* columnist
June 2022

Wherever You Are

Each day this soul becomes more amazed.

—Teresa of Avila, *The Interior Castle*

TWO DECADES AGO, I attended college just outside Chicago. The student body was geographically quite diverse, full of young adults from all fifty states and multiple countries besides. For this reason, many of the welcome-to-a-liberal-arts-institution mixers focused on our places of origin.

"Where are you from?" we'd be invited to ask one another, or "Tell me about your hometown," or, in one ill-conceived instance, "Sit at the lunch table designated for your state!" (There was only one guy from Wyoming, and oh my word, that giant group of Texans was SO LOUD.) For some students, this question was easy to answer. They'd lived in the same town their entire lives until launching off to college. For others it was a little more complicated—Cleveland and *then* Binghamton, New York; San Diego *until* their parents' divorce, and after that, Seattle.

Then there were those who would pause, get a little glassy-eyed, and admit they weren't sure how to even begin answering the question. "Military brat or pastor's kid?" became the running joke, since both the military and the ministry tended to move a family from place to place without time to settle for long.

Where is your home? Is home a place where you've always lived, somewhere you long for, or just the spot you lay your head to rest tonight? What *makes* a home? Why do we sometimes yearn for home and other times feel we will go crazy if we don't leave it? What might it mean to be *at home* no matter where we are?

My husband Daryl and I are raising three pastors' kids ourselves these days. Nearly a decade ago, when we completed background checks as part of our hiring process at the California church we currently serve, we realized we'd moved six times in ten years. Since our wedding, we'd lived on both coasts, in the Midwest, and in the South.

"A stopover in Colorado and we'd have a BINGO," I told him.

"That isn't really how it works," he said. This is his default response when I tell him stuff like "Our printer is out of lasers."

Though we were proud that we'd learned to pack up our entire kitchen in an hour without breaking a glass, we were also very tired. Exhausted, really. The constant ache of jusssssst beginning to grow roots and then discovering we'd need to pull them up time and time again, leaving a piece of our hearts behind with a church and friends and colleagues, was wearing on both of us. These big, painful pieces were the most obvious, but there were also hundreds of micro-stresses involved each time we relocated: finding a new doctor and dentist and mechanic; learning the rhythms of a different local culture; discovering through a series of subtle faux pas that it's pronounced *Loo-ville,* not Looie-ville, or that no one wears high heels to a graveside service during the rainy season in farm country because you will sink right into the lawn, lose a shoe, and end up leading the closing prayers while standing on one foot. (Not that this has ever happened to me, you understand. At least not more than twice.)

Our edges had become so ragged they were more fringe than fabric, so Daryl and I made a pact to try and make a go of it—a real, honest go—this time. To do the necessary deep work to stay in one place for a decade or longer. To be all in, right here, right now. To practice presence right now, *in* the present, to put it in a more whimsical way. With our graduate school and ministerial training finally complete, nothing would push us to move on except us. Or God. (Always a possible spoiler, the Almighty.) Three years in, at a career inflection point, we doubled down. Then, mid-pandemic, watching so many colleagues around the country pull

Present is an invitation to be all here, right where we are, wherever that is, for as long as God invites.

up their anchors, leave their calls, or start over in new places, we committed ourselves once again to the community in front of us. Like Ruth and Naomi, we wanted *these* people to be *our* people, their landscape to be our landscape, and their God to be ours, too. We wanted to be here, and in committing to one place, to find our being here.

This is not at all a word of judgment against anyone who has recently moved or needs to do so soon. Each of us must listen to the siren song of God, and our particular story and callings will, of course, differ from yours. *Present* is, instead, an invitation to be all here, right where we are, wherever that is, for as long as God invites.

Rootedness

There is deep biblical precedent for committing to people and place. Rootedness is a sign of blessing, an intentionality that reflects the favor of God. After the second Advent of Jesus, one of the signs of the fulfillment of God's kingdom will be the restful permanence of God's people. Nomads no longer, they will finally be able to enjoy the fruits of their labor. Jeremiah puts it this way:

> *Again you will plant vineyards*
> *on the hills of Samaria;*
> *the farmers will plant them*
> *and enjoy their fruit.*[1]

Unlike the captives and the exiles—or even Jesus himself, who had nowhere to lay his head—God's resurrected people will be invited to settle in permanently to the new creation. In these homes, war and famine will never threaten, job transfers won't exist, and borders won't separate families. We will, at last—at long, long last—be a people at rest.

Early in the school year, our middle son, Wilson, came home telling us of a classmate who moved away. Tears in his eyes, he curled into Daryl's lap and said, "I didn't even have a chance to get to know her yet!" These separations hurt, no matter our age. My great-grandmother lived to be one hundred and three, and near the end of her life often lamented, "All my friends are dead!" There is a great deal of unavoidable separation baked into life already. Knowing this, shouldn't we do all that's in our power to be all in where we are while we can?

> Rootedness is a sign of blessing, an intentionality that reflects the favor of God.

Extending from the biblical witness (which we will dig into in depth shortly), there is a deep and longstanding Christian tradition of stability, beginning with the first monastics in the early centuries after the death and resurrection of Jesus and continuing on to today. We haven't talked much about it in the contemporary western church; we often prefer the next new and exciting thing over the slow, quiet wisdom of the ancient tradition. This is starting to shift, and I'm so happy to see it. The idea of faithful stability is not novel, but it is, perhaps, one whose time is coming again in greater awareness and fullness. If this book can be even a small part of that reawakening, I will be forever grateful.

The Beginning

Six years ago, Daryl and I prayerfully decided to stop looking up and around and commit to *this* place. To *these* people. A year ago, we recommitted to it all once again. In doing so, we found our lives transformed. In a world marked by transience, envy, and rootlessness, committing to staying put is a radical, unusual act. Choosing stability can seem boring or easy; inertia is a powerful force, after all. But the truth is, there is tremendous growth on offer when we stop holding a community at arms' length and open ourselves to the blessing of stability, the grace of limits, and the joy of presence. This book is divided into sections around these three gifts, each of which comes with our increased attention to being all in—fully present, right where we are.

> God calls us to stability, but never to stay in situations where our spiritual, emotional, or physical health is at risk.

Before we go on, however, I must add one important caveat. There is a time to seek stability, and there is a time when God will call us onward. We can parse the details of when to take that job offer in another city or retire to the Florida panhandle or help plant a new church far from our current abode. Stability's opposite is *instability*, not thoughtful movement. God calls Abraham to leave his homeland and then to stay in a new land for a long time. God inspires Ruth to follow Naomi across borders and cultures. God pushes Paul from his comfortable home in Tarsus to Philippi, Corinth, and Thessalonica. These are matters for prayer, discernment, and wisdom. It is not always God's call to stay put.

And there are still other times when we *must* go: when remaining in one place would expose us to harm or abuse. Hear me plainly: If your spouse or partner is violent toward you, it is time to go. If your church seeks to silence or control you rather than shepherd and care for you, it's likely God will call you to find a new ecclesial home. In instances like these, the virtue of stability has been broken by the malevolence of others. Please check out the resources listed in the endnotes for help in getting out safely.[2] God calls us to stability, but never to stay in situations where our spiritual, emotional, or physical health is at risk. This is not stability, but bondage. God calls us to freedom.

Of course, even aside from instances of abuse, trauma, or neglect, not all instability is chosen. The majority is either unexpected or thrust upon us. You may be serving in the military, attending school, or working in a profession that is known for moving its employees around. Or perhaps you *love* being on the go and bristle at the idea of growing roots when wings seem much more fun. I hear you. Yet even if one of these describes you, I'd argue that being fully where you are *right now*, even if it's only for a few months or weeks, can itself be profoundly transforming. There's a significant psychological difference between living out of a suitcase and putting those clothes into bureau drawers, even if you know you may need to pack them up again soon. In a way, it takes even more courage to press in to a local community if you know you'll be leaving it—and it can bring about some powerful growth and goodness, even in a short time. More on that to come.

For now, let's begin with some full disclosure: I'm writing this book from Southern California. Orange County, to be particular. Home of ridiculously nice weather, killer tacos, and enough outdoor activities to please surfers, swimmers, and hikers alike.

Yesterday my neighbor, who works for a Huge-but-Not-to-Be-Named coffee chain, dropped two pounds of medium roast on my doorstep just because. We are growing clementines *in our backyard*. We *have* a backyard.

"Sure," you might say, "easy for *you* to find contentment where you are. *I* live somewhere *very* different. *I* can't drive to the beach in under an hour. *I* live surrounded by snow/floods/deer ticks/sirens/famine/neighbors with wind chime collections."

Fair enough.

I do love California. It's not a hard place to love. Despite its admitted excesses (we recently endured a recall election of our governor with options on the ballot that included a one-named starlet whose only qualification was "entertainer," and I just ... I can't), it's hard to argue with orange groves and constant sunshine.

But here's the thing: I grew up in northern Wisconsin. Few places in America feel as far removed from those wild, snowy forests and loon-studded lakes as my manicured, roasting, palm-tree-lined suburb. By September each year, I am practically vibrating with a near-constant ache for autumns where I might breathe crisp, apple-y air instead of choking wildfire smoke. I miss the solitude, the small towns, the pace of life more contemplative than constantly on the go. I miss the cost of living being plausible and not utterly bonkers. I miss not knowing anyone who had their sweet-sixteen party on a yacht.

Don't get me wrong, I'm grateful to be here in California. I wouldn't trade it. I'm doing the spiritual work to be all in, right here for a long time, not because the place or its people are perfect—no place is heaven short of, well, heaven. There is not a location on this earth that doesn't have its share of troubles, nor a people, nor a culture. That's part of the transience trap—believing that being somewhere else would finally *complete* us when really, the struggle is within us. As Abba Moses, one of the Desert Fathers, once encouraged a discontented pilgrim, "Go, sit in your cell, and your cell will teach you everything."[3]

Present began as a personal project. I wanted to learn this new way of being for myself. After years of transitional living, I was desperate to find a way to stay put. But even as Daryl and I made plans to hunker down for the long haul, I knew I could be quite capable of living in the same place—for months (years, even!)—without ever truly committing to it. Many of us live with one foot out the door of the home in which God has placed us, our eyes not meeting those of our neighbors but instead searching beyond their shoulders for the greener pastures that might lie just beyond. I was committed to learning, but first I had a whole slew of bad habits that needed to be undone. Habits of biding my time, of pulling back and away, of staying disconnected. Habits of trying to see what might be next any time I grew the tiniest bit discontent with what was right in front of me. When we fail to assume the longevity of place or relationship,

> When we fail to assume the longevity of place or relationship, it is far too easy to take all sorts of unhealthy shortcuts.

it is far too easy to take all sorts of unhealthy shortcuts. We avoid conflict rather than courageously working it through. We let our homes fall into disrepair rather than get out our tools to fix and polish. We allow weeds to creep into the garden, hoping the labor to remove them will fall to the next person in line. I wanted to undo these bad habits, to find a new path; but to be honest, I wasn't even sure where to start.

Learning to be present is a great adventure, an avenue to deeper fellowship with God and our neighbors.

Yet even as I began standing at the shore of this new ocean of possibility, I was suddenly thrown into scarily deep waters. The pandemic locked down California overnight, and suddenly my circle of in-person contacts shrunk to a masked handful. Not only were we not going to move away anytime soon, we weren't even going on *vacation*. With all of my speaking engagements and conferences canceled, I watched my life constrict to our home, our street, our local park. I expected to feel trapped—and at times, I did. I expected to feel afraid—and at times, I did. But even as we grieved, living through a long season of uncertainty and suffering, I discovered new depths to God's love through the gift of the present. We do not serve a God who is far off, but one made incarnate in Jesus Christ, present to us by the Holy Spirit right here, right now, no matter what is swirling around us. God is our rock, tethering us to the present out of love.

As to my own story, after years of transience and instability, I'm working to stay right here, right where I am: not because my place is perfect, but because I've come to believe that the present is a gift. I don't know what the future holds for my little family of five. Even in the long months between the writing and the publication of this book, God may move us somewhere new. But my heart and hope is that this lesson is one I'll be allowed to learn for a very long time to come.

So how can we be *here,* wherever our *here* happens to be? Whether you'll only be in one place for a few weeks or you've never left your town of birth, join me in a celebration and exploration of all things stable, limited, and local as we seek to follow Jesus to the ends of the earth by sitting with him right here at home, enjoying the blessing of stability, the grace of limits, and the joy of presence.

My prayer, dear reader, is that this book might serve as a companion to you as you connect more deeply with this God, too. Learning to be present is a great adventure, an avenue to deeper fellowship with God and our neighbors, and a call to each of us to open our hands and accept the gift.

It's a profoundly good one.

Don't let it pass you by.

Questions for the Present

1

Where is home for you? Is that a difficult or an easy question to answer?

2

Read Jeremiah 31:1–5. How does this passage impact your idea of home?

3

When you think of home, what emotions arise for you?

4

Do you struggle to be still? Why or why not?

5

How might being present right where you are be a spiritual practice?

PART I

The Blessing of Stability

If your life is backwards, you must die before you can live.

—PAUL J. PASTOR, *The Listening Day*

CHAPTER 1

Death to Ferns

It's not magic. It's work.

—Andrew Peterson, *Adorning the Dark*

I KILL A LOT of plants.

I don't mean to, of course. When I bring them home from the nursery in their lacquered pots, I know the plans I have for them, and those plans are good.

Plans to water them the precise amount they need; plans to mist their leaves, to check for disease, to turn them around so their stems grow straight instead of leaning too far toward the window. With apologies to the Lord and Jeremiah, I have plans to prosper and not to harm them. I carry out these plans faithfully for two or three whole days, and then I forget that my plants are in fact natural beings, alive and in need of attention, and I fail to notice them again until they are much too far gone for salvation.

There are many reasons for this, from basic moral failings (Sloth! Pride! Addiction to bad television!) to the realities of parenting that sometimes move too quickly for a meal at the dinner table, much less a check of soil pH levels. Perhaps I buy the wrong plants from the wrong nurseries. For sure I don't pay enough attention to where the sunlight reaches the shelves.

But I believe the real reason is this: For years, Daryl and I moved and moved and moved again, barely unpacking the last of our boxes before filling them with dishes and curtains once more. I couldn't keep even a window garden of herbs because planting seeds without any hope of staying put long enough for the harvest is an exercise in futility. So now, finally trying again in a home we've owned for years, I find I've lost the skill.

The new heavens and the new earth will be marked by stability. No longer will people live in exile, strangers in a strange land.

Our friends Jonathan and Jessica own a brilliant design firm in Los Angeles. The first thing I always notice about their home is its indoor greenery. It's lush with ferns and succulents and Ficus trees.

"Don't ever plant a Ficus outdoors," Jonathan tells me. "Even if you plant it in a highway median, these things are ferocious. Its roots can tear up asphalt." Their home feels alive, organic. I can practically taste the oxygen filtered through the ubiquitous leaves. The air feels fresher indoors than out. Whenever I visit, I want to stay forever. Jonathan and Jessica know how to tend to tender greens; their attention doesn't waver after a day or two. I was sort of hoping some of their skill would rub off on me, but so far, no dice.

The book of Isaiah speaks of the hallmark of the coming Kingdom of God, that the new heavens and the new earth will be marked by stability. No longer will people live in exile, strangers in a strange land. Instead they will sow and reap, plant and harvest, enjoying the fruits of their labors. Writes Isaiah:

They will build houses and dwell in them;
  they will plant vineyards and eat their fruit.
No longer will they build houses and others live in them,
  or plant and others eat.
For as the days of a tree,
  so will be the days of my people;
my chosen ones will long enjoy
  the work of their hands.[4]

This blessing will be a sign of God's triumph over death and evil, a mark of final victory. This is our dream, our hope, our anticipated reality in the kingdom to come. At the end, when all is said and done, our reward is restful presence in a beautiful, stable place, rooted in peace with God and our neighbors. Yet tastes of this blessing are also offered to us right now, today, albeit in less polished form.

We are invited to partake of the blessing of stability.

This blessing is a hard one to lay hold of in our hypermobile, ever-distracted culture. Many of us relocate often, or we travel for work, or we are constantly on the lookout for the next best opportunity, no matter where it might take us. Even if we don't leave our towns of residence, we keep our eyes open for a church with a better program, a school with richer arts offerings or a stronger soccer team, a new restaurant to check out rather than our old standby. Sure, that old standby might close without our business, but what's that to us? Like sharks, we must keep swimming, lest we die.

The transient nature of our current culture is illustrated in what's becoming a necessity in fire-ravaged California. Here we are encouraged by the local authorities to have a "go bag" at the ready stuffed with essential supplies. A few bottles of water, a first aid kit, any necessary medications. Those with tiny kids are reminded to pack diapers or formula. Don't forget some nonperishable food, a flashlight, a battery-powered radio—and extra batteries. Disaster could strike at any moment, so it's wise to be prepared. People living in places prone to hurricanes or flooding might keep a similar stash at the ready. Those living in war-torn areas likely maintain a mental inventory of what to grab if hiding or flight becomes necessary.

When smoke curls over the horizon, I check our stock of supplies in case we need to hit the road in a hurry. We evacuated once for nearly a week, piling into the car to take refuge at our friends' home an hour south, the kids thrilled for the adventure of it all, me just grateful to have air clean enough to breathe, Daryl taking church phone calls in Michelle and Kevin's backyard, surrounded by chickens and beehives.

When we went back home again, after the smoke had cleared and the firefighters worked their magic, we did laundry and aired out the house and repacked our go bags with things we discovered we'd missed—contact solution and toothbrushes, and a couple of travel games because bored children invite their own unique types of disaster. ("Look, mom! My seatbelt is so tangled up it doesn't work anymore!") We live ready to leave in haste.

This shapes us, body, mind, and spirit. To exist perched on the edge of our metaphorical seats, ready to run, to spring into action, to go, go, *go,* is profoundly unsettling. Though there are dozens of biblical stories of God calling people far afield— Abraham and Moses, Miriam and Esther, Peter and Barnabas and Paul—there are just as many stories of staying put. But these are rarely as glamorous.

Take Anna, the prophetess from Luke 2, for example. After seven brief years of marriage, she is widowed. For the entire rest of her life—decades—she goes to the Temple to fast and pray. We aren't told her hopes or dreams, but surely many of them were shattered in her husband's death.

To exist perched on the edge of our metaphorical seats, ready to run, to spring into action, to go, go, go, is profoundly unsettling.

Without status or family, she goes to the only place she knows she will always be welcomed: into the house of God. She spends her days quietly, faithfully attentive to the Lord. On the surface, there is nothing to this story: no plot, no conflict, no thread. Just simple, repeated faithfulness. Sacred dependence. Holy obedience.

Until the day half a century later when Anna holds in her arms the salvation of the world. The blessing of stability.

God may call each of us to go and do and leave and travel. Daryl and I have these stories ourselves—clear leading from God, miles beneath our wheels, lessons learned. But God calls us most often to be *still,* knowing and trusting in the divine presence here and now. Quietly, faithfully working in the small, mundane, sacred ordinary right here. Right now. This is a tough assignment when we feel such an inner drive to keep at least one eye on the shifting winds.

Transience threatens to dull our awareness of God, flattening our soul's attention to the more subtle signs of the Spirit. This is troubling because God tends to come to us in gentleness—a baby, born in a manger; a still, small voice; a divine nudge; a soft knock at the door. St. Teresa of Avila wrote of the necessity to cultivate spiritual attention, a quieting of the heart and mind in order to discern the voice and love of God. For her, God's presence unfolded slowly, a journey into the heart of a castle with many rooms, many distractions, many twists and turns. But at the divine center: glory. How much truer do her words ring on this side of the digital age!

Ready to Stay

Before kids, Daryl and I once spent a few nights a week crashing at a friend's home to save us the two-hour commute to and from our unpaid internship. The friend worked long hours, so we didn't see much of him. Exhausted from our long days, we ate a lot of prepackaged smoothies and take-out pizza, but occasionally we'd cook something. It proved tricky in a kitchen still filled with boxes.

"Is he moving?" I asked Daryl.

"He's been here for years," he said, "but I don't think he's decided whether he's going to stay."

This friend lived ready to leave, uncertain about his next steps. I've lived this way myself. Perhaps you have, too. Perhaps you are right there today.

It's tough to grow if we are ready to leave at any moment. Like a plant torn from the soil too many times, shallow roots stunt spiritual health, longevity, and maturity. Will we work through conflict with a friend or a neighbor if we're about to move away? Nah, we'll be gone soon anyway. Should we invest in caring for our home? Probably not, if we won't be living in it for long. Will we plant herbs or vegetables or flowers? Not if we won't be here for the harvest. In the short term, transience looks as though it will solve a host of problems, but if we dig a little deeper, it becomes clear that it tends to cause far more issues than it resolves, and that these are often much bigger.

In his book *Endurance,* Alfred Lansing chronicles Ernest Shackleton's ill-fated attempt to reach the South Pole. Though they faced some bumps at the start of the expedition, outlooks remained sunny. Notes Lansing, "Underlying the optimism and good spirits of the party was a deep-seated confidence that their situation was only temporary."[5] However, their journey, scheduled to take only short months in reasonable weather, ended up taking far longer in devastatingly terrible conditions.

Shackleton soon realized that simmering conflicts between crew members that could have been smoothed over with better sailing and a shorter-term expedition would need dealing with—and fast. He dove into the hard work of making peace—or at least a ceasefire between two of his more cantankerous and volatile crew members—and it is his leadership that the team credited with the entire crew's ultimate survival against nearly impossible odds.

Of course, stability is not always our choice to make. Some of us serve companies that require travel or relocation without giving us much say. Sometimes duty to family in a time of need requires uprooting. The call of God may ask us to serve in a new place. Plus, there's the hard truth that we increasingly live in a world of refugees and immigrants, unsafe homes and homelands. This book is not a treatise on why any of the reasons we might need to get up and go are bad or wrong or ill-advised. Instead, it is a call to be fully present where we are, right now. If that place can be cultivated for the long term, all the better; but if it truly cannot, then living well in the moments we have where we are is a profoundly worthwhile practice. Let us *be here now*, present in the present to the present.

> **Like a plant torn from the soil too many times, shallow roots stunt spiritual health, longevity, and maturity.**

An Ancient Practice

A few years ago, pastor and professor Dennis Okholm delivered a guest sermon at our church on the spiritual discipline of stability. I'd never heard of such a thing. In all my years of churchgoing I'd listened to dozens of sermons about following God wherever he leads—even to the ends of the earth! I'd heard missionaries tell adventurous tales of leaving home and hearth behind. I'd searched the Scriptures myself and found inspiration for my own seminary journey in the story of Isaiah—"Here I am, send me!"—and in moving to California in the story of Abraham, leaving the familiar behind. No one had ever spoken from the pulpit about the blessing of stability and God's call to some or even most of us to remain right where we are planted and work to be faithful right here. I left Sunday worship excited to learn more.

It turns out there's a long-standing Christian tradition beginning with the monastics in the second and third centuries that's centered around the simple practice of staying put. For some, this meant a cloistered life dedicated to God within the confines of a monastery. Notes Rich Villodas, "Monks who enter a monastery take a vow of stability that grounds them in certain places for life." Even then, among men of such holiness, there were petty grievances and near-daily frustrations. People, after all, are always people. Yet "in a commitment to stability, we withstand the disturbances and annoyances of others for the sake of union with God and union with each other."[6] Other monastics would dedicate just a season or a number of years to one particular place and group of people. For all, it meant acquiescing to the challenges and embracing the blessings of remaining present wherever God had placed them, even with the monotonies, irritations, and constraints a particular place invariably entails.

I wanted to learn more about this whole idea. I *needed* to learn more about it. If Daryl and I were indeed to stay put in our current location with our little family, we would need to embrace a whole new skill set. After years of hypermobility in a culture that celebrates hypermobility, we wanted to drink deeply from the well of stability's blessings. Yet if I couldn't keep a houseplant alive on the windowsill, even the succulent that Jonathan promised me was *very difficult* to murder, I wondered if there was any hope for me at all.

So I began where I always do when I'm fresh out of hope.

I went to the Scriptures.

Coming Home

The ultimate call to each one of us in Scripture is to come home. Home is where God is, a place of safety and presence, feast and blessing and rest. When we think of home, those of us with positive, nostalgic childhoods may remember gathering around a table for meals, the warmth of an embrace, a feeling of acceptance or happiness or peace. Those of us with rockier upbringings may find within ourselves a sense of loss and longing—we know what home *should* have been or *could* have been, and we yearn for that simple, joyful safety, love, and rest.

God promises us a home with him where every tear will be wiped away, shattered souls and lives will be made whole, and God himself will live among us—we as his people, God as our God. The book of Revelation paints a picture of a people at rest, enjoying rich feasts, at peace with God, one another, and themselves.[7] This is the fulfillment we long for, the pinnacle of our salvation. As Sally Lloyd-Jones puts it in her *Jesus Storybook Bible*, because of Jesus "the sad things come untrue."[8] We hope and look and long for this perfection, this consummation.

But we must not stop here. The Christian life is not solely about hoping, longing, and waiting for eternity. Followers of Jesus have gotten themselves—and entire systems and societies—in heaps of trouble by promoting eternal salvation without a mention of earthly good. If our hope is *only* in this eternal reality and has nothing to say to the injustices, sufferings, and disorders of our time, we would be better off in medically induced comas until glory. Instead, Scripture paints a profound and compelling picture of the age to come, while *also* calling us to work for the kingdom here and now. Future blessing must not lull us into complacency while we wait. There is work—good work, sacred work—to be done. And much of this work centers around stability.

> Scripture paints a profound and compelling picture of the age to come, while *also* calling us to work for the kingdom here and now.

Scripture offers three beautiful metaphors for the stability into which God invites us: cisterns (or wells), houses, and vineyards. We will take each one in turn.

Questions for the Present

1

How many times in your life have you moved?
Which time was easiest? Hardest?

2

What is one problem moving away might solve?
What is one problem it might create?

3

What does Courtney mean by "the blessing of
stability"? How does God meet us in stillness?

4

Read Isaiah 65:20–24. How is stability presented as a
future hope? Which part feels most alluring to you?

5

What is your greatest challenge in
seeking stability right now?

CHAPTER 2

Drawn to the Well

Rivers of living water will brim
and spill out of the depths
of anyone who believes in me this way.

—John 7:38, *The Message*

I KEEP FRIENDS above my writing desk, and by friends, I mean books by authors I love and admire. Flannery O'Connor is there, as are a host of white American dudes recognizable by just their last names—Steinbeck, Salinger, Saunders, Irving, Eggers, McCarthy.

There are the breathtaking contemporary novelists—Jesmyn Ward, James Baldwin, Jhumpa Lahiri, Lisa See, Shusaku Endo. There's my beloved nonfiction section, shelves of writers who pastor me across time and space—Fleming Rutledge, Anne Lamott, Wendell Berry, Esau McCaulley, Rich Villodas, Eugene Peterson, Brenda Salter McNeil, C. S. Lewis, Dietrich Bonhoeffer, Martin Luther King Jr.

Then there's the watercolor art print, gifted to me by fellow author Catherine McNiel, that quotes Julian of Norwich.

"All shall be well," it says. "And all shall be well, and all manner of things shall be well."

"Do you promise?" I yelled at it during the pandemic, news of a friend's death trembling in my voice. *"Well? Really?!"*

I rearrange my writing desk often, removing piles of peanut butter cup wrappers, replacing sources I've scoured with new ones fresh from the library, but the quote always remains. On good days, I believe it. On bad ones, I hate it. On all days, it brings me to wonder: What does *well* look like? Surely to be *well* is more than to be free from illness. Wellness is flourishing health—body, mind, and soul.

And then there is its lovely homonym: the well as a cistern.

* * *

Daryl dug postholes in our backyard a couple of years ago, four feet deep and twelve inches across. He borrowed a manual posthole digger from a friend who told him a motorized one would be too tricky in our small, rock-studded space. When Daryl came in for a glass of water after digging his first hole, I asked whether he'd accidentally turned the sprinklers on.

"No," he said. "Why?"

"Well, did you step into the shower or something?" I asked.

"Court, this is *sweat*."

Digging is serious business, especially in a hot climate. You want that work to *count*. While digging those postholes, Daryl discovered new compassion for anyone who's ever had to dig for a living, new understanding of the toll physical labor can take, and new gratitude for our modern-day systems of plumbing.

Water is *everything*. A healthy adult can survive for upwards of forty days without food, but only two or three without water. Animals will put their lives on the line to visit a watering hole—braving crocodiles or piranha for a sip of essential refreshment, knowing instinctively that the risk of quick-and-painful-death-by-predator is preferable to the certainty of a long, agonizing death-by-dehydration.

In the near-desert climate of Southern California, children are so well taught in the importance of regularly sipping from their reusable water bottles that by age two, our oldest used to lecture us to "Keep drinking so you don't get na-ny-a-gated!"—his knowledge of proper hydration vastly outpacing his pronunciation. Without a consistent source of fresh water, no one can survive, much less stay put for long. Our biblical forebears knew this, which is one reason they dedicated so much text to the importance of water and all the metaphors therein.

In Genesis 26, we find Isaac facing a famine. He ponders heading down to Egypt, where there might be more food, but then he receives a word from the Lord that he should remain where he is.

God tells Isaac, "Stay in this land for a while, and I will be with you and will bless you."[9] So Isaac settles in, trusting that God will sustain him. He uncovers the wells dug by his father, Abraham, to provide water for his animals, and God keeps his promise:

Isaac's wells draw abundant water. They provide so much, in fact, that Isaac soon incurs the jealousy of the Philistines, whose animals aren't doing nearly as well in the season of famine. They fill in his wells—the ultimate petty grudge move—so he responds by traveling a little farther onward and uncovering more wells his father once dug. They also fill in *those* wells—people haven't changed much in a few thousand years, have they?—so now, out of ancient wells to uncover, Isaac digs his own. One final cistern.

> Stability is never without opposition. Whatever place God calls us to inhabit will have its share of challenges.

They leave this one alone: whether because they've gotten worn out chasing Isaac across the arid countryside, because God intervenes, or for another reason entirely, we don't know. The text doesn't say. Isaac names this final well *Rehoboth,* which means "room," grateful to finally have the space to stay put.

This Genesis story is about staying in one place, but it's also paradoxically about moving on. At first Isaac digs a well, but then he is not allowed to use it, so he moves a little farther away and digs again, and again the same thing happens. God tells him to "stay in this land," and then the people of that land drive him away. Stability is never without opposition. Whatever place God calls us to inhabit will have its share of challenges. We experience wildfires here; East Coasters face hurricanes; a dear friend weathered violent protests outside her apartment door in Washington, DC; my parents in Wisconsin saw massive trees ripped up by their roots during a recent tornado. Isaac's famine is just one disaster in a long line of them. There will be more. There are always more.

Beyond the natural disasters, Isaac faces the struggle of living among a people who do not welcome him. To them he is a foreigner and a stranger; he worships an unfamiliar God, practices unfamiliar customs, speaks an unfamiliar language. Yet his story is illustrative even for those of us who live in the same towns in which we were born. To be a human is to be a sojourner, even among our own people. It is even more painful to watch a loved one fill in our freshly dug well than it is to have a stranger do the same.

Yet God's word to Isaac remains true and clear: "Stay for a while." The days for this project are not numbered or given. Thus the instruction also becomes an invitation to trust, to watch and wait and pray and listen for the next round of God's call and instructions. Isaac pitches his tent and digs his well—his *Rehoboth*, his *Room-Enough*—and waits.

The Allure of Living Water

Years ago I heard a speaker (whose name I've forgotten) illustrate two ways churches tend to shepherd their people. The first is by building fences to keep people contained. There are dangers outside the sheepfold, after all—predators and rushing rivers and vast wilderness. The fences are built upon a belief in the importance of safeguarding vulnerable sheep, and also upon the teaching that Christians should be set apart from the secular culture. In less benevolent circumstances, fences are sometimes built because of us-versus-them theology or fear of the outside world. In practice, fences tend to look like a lot of "no." *We don't listen to that music. Our kids don't go to that school. We are against this and that and the other thing.* Fence churches often lean into the culture wars, defining themselves in large part by what they are against.

The true danger of fences arrives when we seek to consume only that which fits into a reduced Christian subculture—one that may even take on unhealthy elements of nationalism. When we limit our social structures to only what is inside the fence, we often end up with impoverished imaginations and a reduced capacity to love those on the margins or the outside. If we don't know anyone "out there" very well, it will be hard to love anyone not already in our pasture. If we don't love them, we will struggle to invite them to join us inside. A lack of love often breeds distrust, fear, anger, and outright hostility.

Love, on the other hand, casts out fear. Love walks hand in hand with humility, acknowledging the dignity and worth of the outsider: not as a prize to be claimed or a number to be counted (or an enemy to be attacked!), but as a person in their own right, with gifts to share and wisdom to offer. Jesus was a master of this type of love. It was often the outsiders who welcomed him first and best—fishermen, children, tax collectors, sinners.

Southern Baptist professor and scholar Karen Swallow Prior recently wrote a series of introductions to classic works of literature. There were some of the usual suspects—*Pride and Prejudice*, for one—containing nothing even most Victorian grandmothers would find objectionable. But she didn't stop with straightforward classics. She also wrote prefaces to *Frankenstein* and Joseph Conrad's *Heart of Darkness.*

"We are tethered to the eternal rock," she told Phil Vischer on an episode of *The Holy Post Podcast.* "With that certainty, I don't understand why we don't feel free to explore."[10] I still remember the joy and relief I felt my first semester as an undergraduate at Wheaton College when I discovered we'd be reading authors like Annie Dillard and Langston Hughes and George Saunders. I'd worried we'd be limited to explicitly Christian fiction, a subgenre often—but not always—reduced to platitudes and two-dimensional characters rather than deep and nuanced expressions of humanity.

I fell so deeply in love with the truth and beauty of literature that I headed out to study it in graduate school, too. The school I attended was loosely Jesuit, but my professors ran the faith gamut from atheist to agnostic to Protestant to Buddhist. When I wrote a paper on John Steinbeck's *East of Eden*, one of my senior professors, a lapsed Catholic, called me into his office.

"This is a fine paper," he said. "It's well-written, and you've earned an A. However, you should know that it isn't really a literature paper."

I blanched. It wasn't?

"You've written a theology paper," he told me, handing it back. I began to sputter.

"But … but I don't *do* theology!" I exclaimed.

"If you say so," he said. "But you may want to think about studying it. You seem to have a knack." It was his word of reorientation that began shaping my understanding of what theology could be. It was a study of Scripture and philosophy and church tradition, yes, but it was also a study of the story of God in every other story in the world, from Steinbeck to Shelley to Stephen King. The gate to my fence had been opened, and it turned out God was waiting out there, too.

A New and Ancient Way

Perhaps we need not build fences. Perhaps there is a better way. That speaker years ago offered a second metaphor to describe what the church could be. "Instead of fences," he said, "we can dig wells." Living water draws people in. It is alluring and enticing because it is *good*. Plus, wells don't force people to abide by arbitrary bounds. (I know I wasn't the only elder Millennial who snapped her secular CDs in half *for Jesus*. I'm so sorry, Savage Garden.) When Paul shows up in Athens, he doesn't begin by saying, "You all are pagans and need to start watching only Veggie Tales." (And don't get me wrong—I love me some VT!) Instead, he looks and sees and seeks to understand their culture from the inside out. Then, discovering a particular statue, he finds his way in:

> If we dig good wells that burst forth with fresh water, we will have no need for fences.

As I walked around and looked carefully at your objects of worship, I even found an altar with this inscription:

TO AN UNKNOWN GOD. So you are ignorant of the very thing you worship—and this is what I am going to proclaim to you.

The God who made the world and everything in it is the Lord of heaven and earth and does not live in temples built by human hands.[11]

Paul proclaims the gospel and the freedom of Christ's call to live in a new way, unbound by the fear of retribution from their pagan gods. Water draws in. Fences keep out. Love draws in. Fear keeps out.

If we dig good wells that burst forth with fresh water, we will have no need for fences. The living water Christ offers is its own invitation, a clarion call to come and receive divine, eternal refreshment. In fact, in addition to building hurdles in our lives of faith and imagination, erecting unnecessary fences can actually end up keeping people *out*. Jesus has some harsh words for anyone who would stand in the way of a lost sheep coming home.

●　●　●

On a drive to school recently, my oldest son asked what would happen if he didn't believe all the right things about Jesus. His question pierced me deeply, since it's one I wrestle with myself.

"Do you know those basket thingies that helicopters use to rescue people?" I asked him.

"Yeah," he said, "the ones that hang down on a long cable?"

"Right. Well, we are drowning in the ocean, and Jesus is like a rescue swimmer who comes to save us. And sometimes we've had too much saltwater to drink, or we're really exhausted and scared, and so Jesus loads us into that basket. And we might say, 'Jesus, I don't believe this rope even exists!' And then Jesus might say, 'That's okay. I've still got you.'"

My son paused, his brow furrowed in the same crease that's become permanently etched in my own.

"Am I drowning?" he asked.

"We all are," I said. He smiled.

"And God is the Coast Guard!"

"Exactly."

● ● ●

God calls us to dig, but not postholes for a fence. Something better. Something deeper.

Let's dig wells.

Questions for the Present

1

Read Genesis 26:3, 12–22. How would you have felt in Isaac's shoes at the beginning of the story? The middle? The end?

2

Why would God ask Isaac to stay in the land if he knew he'd face such opposition? What lessons might we learn in the struggle?

3

Describe a time you tried to stay put even though it was challenging. How did God meet you in the work?

4

What is the difference between a fence and a well when it comes to drawing people to God?

5

How has your church (if you attend one) taught about drawing people to God? Has it been more about fences (keep things/people out!) or wells (here is living water; join us!)?

CHAPTER 3

Building Houses

I want a home.

—Lucy Ricardo, *Being the Ricardos*

WE WEREN'T ALLOWED to paint the walls of our rented seminary apartments. Normally this wouldn't have bothered me. People have varying tastes, after all, and one person's Perfect Pigeon Grey is another's Totally Depressing Worst Color Ever™. But here's the thing: Those apartment buildings were scheduled to be demolished the year after we graduated. They had pink-tiled bathrooms that appeared straight out of the 1970s because *they were straight out of the 1970s*. The pest-control folks eventually gave up managing the cockroaches because, as one guy told me, "At this point they're pretty well moved in."

But no, we still couldn't paint the walls because, as the administration told us, it was important to create *a culture of not painting*. If they allowed *us* to paint, what would happen when the beautiful, pristine new seminary apartments were built? It'd be Valspar anarchy! Sherwin Williams chaos!

I fought the power for a while before I ran out of steam. Paint Hill wasn't one I was willing to die on, and between trying desperately to learn Hebrew and pretending I didn't notice the cockroaches, I was basically out of energy anyway.

"I'm going to call them beetles," I told Daryl. "That's way less gross. Ladybugs are beetles after all, right?"

"Sure," he said, glancing up from his own Hebrew notes. "Whatever works for you."

After graduation, Daryl and I lived in rentals for years, from sharing a duplex in Nashville with a med-student neighbor happy to share his WiFi (bless you, Faisal), to a historic parsonage in Wisconsin to a tiny condominium in California with such stringent HOA rules our kids weren't allowed sidewalk chalk. We were pretty good tenants—we didn't throw loud parties, we rolled our trash cans in from the curb, we paid on time. (Well, the parsonage was free, since I was the pastor, but you know what I mean.)

In 2017, after years of skimping and saving, plus significant generosity from our church and Daryl's family, we purchased a beautiful little yellow house, and I set to living my ultimate dream—choosing interior paint colors. No more tan or taupe or horrific pink bathroom; it was time for Arctic Sky and Chantilly Lace and Calming Aloe. I love me some cool neutrals!

"Only Benjamin Moore," our interior designer friends told us. "Trust us."

So we painted, with friends from church showing up holding drop cloths and extra brushes and music playlists, climbing on ladders in flip-flops, eating pizza with us on folding chairs in the dust bowl of our unfinished backyard. At one point I poked my head into a bathroom to find a church elder crouched between the vanity and the toilet.

"I'm just going to get this last spot!" she called, her voice muffled by cabinet and plumbing.

That night I lay atop the comforter on our bed and gestured to the walls all around.

"I *love* it," I told Daryl. "I feel like we finally *live* here, you know? We aren't just temporarily stopping by. This is *our* home."

Paint is such a small, simple thing. But even a splash of color can be a visible sign of an invisible grace.

Especially if it's Benjamin Moore.[12]

● ● ●

The second biblical metaphor for stability comes to us from Jeremiah:

> This is what the LORD Almighty, the God of Israel, says to all those I carried into exile from Jerusalem to Babylon: "Build houses and settle down; plant gardens and eat what they produce. Marry and have sons and daughters; find wives for your sons and give your daughters in marriage, so that they too may have sons and daughters. Increase in number there; do not decrease. Also, seek the peace and prosperity of the city to which

I have carried you into exile. Pray to the LORD for it,
because if it prospers, you too will prosper."[13]

God's people will be exiled in Babylon, far from their familiar
landscape and people. Their hearts' desire will be to return to
Jerusalem, to their familiar olive groves and hills and vineyards
and family homes. False prophets are promising them not to
worry, that all these good things will happen soon, that they
should simply bide their time, because *if* God carries them into
exile (and really, why would he do that when they are such great,
obedient people?), God will then bring them home again in a jiffy.

No, says Jeremiah, this is not the case. They will be exiles for
some time, and in their exile, they should settle in for the
long haul.

No doubt this news stung in the ears of those who heard it. In
fact, many chose to ignore Jeremiah's words and instead live
with their metaphorical suitcases packed and donkeys saddled,
ready to return home at any moment. Yet not only does God
instruct the people to prepare to wait patiently, he also tells
them to put down roots. They are to build houses, plant gardens,
marry, and start families. Beyond that, they are not to rail or fight
against the pagan peoples with whom they live, but instead to
seek their good and pray for them. Israel's flourishing during
their exile is directly tied to the flourishing of those with whom
they live—their captors and oppressors.

Whoa.

Building houses and living in them is a blessing for us, of course, freeing us from the unsettledness of needing to move on at any time. But it's also a sign to our neighbors that we want to live our lives among them. As Tish Harrison Warren notes in *Liturgy of the Ordinary*, "When we seek peace, we begin where we are."[14] No longer set apart, no longer planning to leave as soon as we are able, moving into a home means planting a flag in a single place, signaling to ourselves and our neighbors that *this is our place*. It means an acceptance of the blessings and burdens of a particular location, and the people as blessings and burdens that will belong to us, too.

In *Better than Brunch: Missional Churches in Cascadia,* Jason Byassee and Ross A. Lockhart write about Grandview Church in Vancouver: "Churches often think of mission as a program, something you plan and put on the calendar and then do for other people. Grandview shows mission is the whole church's life: living in a way that is different than our neighbors *in order to bless our neighbors*."[15] Building houses in imperfect communities is an act of profound faith and courage. (And when I write "building houses," I do so as a larger metaphor for "living purposefully in a place," whether renting or owning. I realize home ownership is out of reach for many—including my own family, apart from the generosity

> Loving the *idea* of something is rarely useful; it costs us little or nothing. Love is lived in the present—in a place, at a time, with a people.

of our church.) Left to our own devices, we will always be in search of a greener pasture, and in so doing, we may cease to live well at all. It is in choosing to build houses that we begin to find the freedom to seek the peace of our particular city or town or neighborhood. Such work will take time and insight and patience and the knowledge that only living together can bring. As Warren notes,

> In the Christian faith it's almost a philosophical principle that the universal is known through the particular and the abstract through the concrete. We love people universally by loving the particular people we can know and name. We love the world by loving a particular place in it—a specific creek or hill or city or block.[16]

Loving the *idea* of something is rarely useful; it costs us little or nothing. Love is lived in the present—in a place, at a time, with a people.

● ● ●

In fifth grade I just knew I wanted to be a veterinarian when I grew up. I'd read every James Herriot book ever written *twice*. I loved animals. Medicine fascinated me. It was all a done deal—until my parents wisely arranged an opportunity for me to shadow our local vet for a day. Within the first hour, he put a massive German shepherd under anesthesia and sliced into her abdomen. I promptly passed out. Turns out I like the *idea* of veterinary medicine much more than the scalpels-and-blood reality of it all. The proof is in the particulars.

Following Jeremiah's call to "seek the peace of the city" can help us reframe the dangerous and destructive us-and-them themes when we find them in modern Christendom. The exiles in Babylon aren't told to cloister or draw inward, ignoring the pagan peoples around. And before we can argue that perhaps their captors weren't *that bad*, let's remember that Babylon is used repeatedly throughout Scripture as an example of the people *absolutely antithetical* to the one true God. If God's people are the Jedi, Babylon is The Empire. If God's people are hobbits, Babylon is filled with orcs.

Yet God calls his people to press in, even in Babylon. To stay. To love and serve. To build houses.

> God calls his people to press in, even in Babylon. To stay. To love and serve. To build houses.

For us, establishing a home has become about so much more than paint colors. It's getting to know the fears and loves of the neighbors on our cul-de-sac, parsing the unique and kooky culture of Orange County, seeking the flourishing of our public schools and city council and local businesses and fire department and food pantry. It's refusing to live with our metaphorical bags packed, endeavoring to work through conflict when it crops up and to love our community well, even when that community presents challenges.

And it *is* about paint colors, too. Because stability helps teach us to cultivate beauty and hospitality right where we are. And nothing says welcome like Calming Aloe.

Questions for the Present

1

What house do you remember most fondly? Why?

2

Does where you live today feel like home?
Why or why not?

3

Read Jeremiah 29:4–7. What surprises you about
this passage? How might you understand it in light
of the larger arc of Scripture?

4

How does God invite us to practice stability in
seasons of disruption (Jeremiah's exile, for example)?

5

What disruptions do you face today?
Where is God within that struggle?

CHAPTER 4

Planting Vineyards

When we attune to the earth as creatures,
live in harmony with wildness,
and appreciate nature,
we can work toward healing.

—Heidi Barr and Ellie Roscher, *12 Tiny Things*

As I'VE MENTIONED, inside our home is where plants come to die. I don't mean to kill them, I really don't. But ever since I brought home a red geranium to perch on my college dormitory shelf (the school library had one on every windowsill—how hard could they possibly be to keep alive?) I've been a serial murderer of plants. I overwater. I underwater. I can even kill a cactus.

Once a year or so, Daryl drives to the nursery and purchases me a new batch, and I promise to keep an eye on them, to download an app, to put the little indoor watering can right on my nightstand to help jog my memory. And then I kill them all. How do spider mites end up *indoors?* Why is root rot such a *problem?* When did succulents get so *fussy?* I'll never know.

The pots of dried leaves strewn throughout our home stand in stark contrast to our outer landscape, which is lush and green and studded with vegetables and herbs and flowers. Daryl does the yard. He's a wonder with his green thumb and infinite patience for researching natural pest control, watering times, and how to rid the yard of invasive weeds. When a friend or neighbor celebrates a milestone, I often go to the yard with pruning shears and fill up a vase of roses and zinnias and hollyhocks, and each time it feels like a miracle. Each time, I suppose it actually is.

● ● ●

Jeremiah's instructions to the exiles to build houses come with a chaser: They are also to plant vineyards. Unlike an herb garden or a seasonal vegetable patch, vineyards take time to cultivate and develop. It's another way of saying, "You'll be here for some time. Put down roots."

We make different plans when we intend to be somewhere for a while. A one-night hotel stay means we likely won't unpack our suitcase into those bureau drawers, while for a one-month stay we will. A local friend helped us build shade sails in our backyard the first year we lived in our home. Impressed by his building skill, Daryl inquired about his help in erecting solar panels on our roof.

"I'd love to help you do that," he said, "if you're still here in five years." We intend to be. But this kind man has befriended enough pastors in his day to know that ministers can be quite transient.

Along with digging wells and building houses, planting vineyards rooted the people of God to a particular place, helping them to be present, right where they were, tuned in to the rhythms of the seasons and the needs of the land. It takes a vineyard up to a quarter century to hit peak production. Vines require time to cultivate, including a yearly pruning when they are cut back significantly in order to help them produce the best, healthiest fruit in season.

Jeremiah's instructions to plant vineyards roots God's people to the land, but it also connects them more deeply with their neighbors and communities.

When a family from our congregation invited Daryl and the kids and me to visit the vineyard they'd taken on as a retirement project, we jumped at the chance. The property featured rows and rows of Malbec and Sangiovese vines, owl houses to invite nocturnal predators to deal with the gophers, an Airstream trailer for bathroom needs, and a cheery red barn to house tractors and rakes. When our boys heard they'd get to sit on Daryl's lap and help drive the tractors, Wilson practically levitated with excitement. I walked through the fields in the dappled shade of the morning, marveling that such tranquility existed just an hour from the bustle of our busy suburb. Ramona's arid hills reminded me of photos I'd seen of Napa Valley and Italian wine country.

Our friends gave Daryl and me a quick primer on how the vines are planted, grown, and pruned. They hired a vineyard manager to help plant when they founded the vineyard on an empty plot of land, but they oversaw the annual harvests themselves: first four thousand pounds of grapes, then eighteen-five, then nineteen thousand. Caring for a vineyard takes a particular kind of love and attention—left on its own for too long, gophers would chew through roots, weeds would erupt, disease could fester. Growing grapes to harvest requires regular walks up and down the rows, inspecting the soil, watching the weather, adjusting the watering, spreading the mulch.

They told me that when harvest time comes, there's only a short window to cut the grapes from the vines before they spoil. The difference between peak ripeness and overripeness is a hair's breadth.

"Most years, the varieties ripen at different intervals," they told us. "This year, they all happened at once."

"That sounds like a lot," I said.

"It was wonderful," they said. "And boy, we were tired!" During the annual harvests, they often send out an invitation to folks from our church to come and help with the harvest. Many hands make light work, of course, but there's also joy in serving together in a common project, hoisting shears in the beating sun to bring fruit to bins, partaking in the cycle of life and growth and harvest that we miss when we get all our produce from a big-box store. Jeremiah's instructions to God's people to plant vineyards roots them to the land, but it also connects them more deeply with their neighbors and communities. Vineyards require workers or neighbors or friends or volunteers, especially at harvest time.

I asked why they took on such a big project in retirement, and it became clear they loved their home and its land and simply wanted to dig in a little deeper during the third act of their lives.

"We've always had green thumbs," they said. "This is just more of that."

Later that afternoon, as Daryl and I drove home with a gifted bottle of wine and jars of grape preserves clinking lightly in our trunk, harvested from the very vines we'd visited, we asked the kids what they'd want to name a vineyard if we ever owned one.

"Probably Grapetastic," said Lincoln.

"Perfect," said Daryl. "Grapetastic it is."

Tiny Treasures

We have a little apple tree in our front yard, planted over a dozen years ago by a former owner we'll probably never meet. Our house has seen a lot of turnover in its forty years of existence, so we don't know who to thank for the tasty, tart, red-and-green dappled apples we enjoy every October. Daryl and I pruned it last year, and I spent weeks fretting that I'd killed it, too, now adding an outdoor casualty to my streak of indoor plant murders. It looked so sad and stubby and bare, like a teenager after a bad trip to the barbershop. We followed the care instructions that we had googled down to the letter, but things looked dire.

Then, this October, the tree burst forth in the best, biggest fruit we'd seen since we moved in half a decade ago.

"Mom!" Lincoln came running in from the front yard holding a softball-sized apple. "LOOK AT THIS!"

Pruning nearly always looks too severe. When grapevines are pruned in the off-season—somewhere between January and February here in California—the remaining plants look woody and anemic. Stripped of their shoots and leaves, they appear nearly dead. Then the spring comes, and slowly, new green shoots appear, snaking up through the wires and nets designed to give them support. Buds and leaves sprout, and then blossoms and fruit. Without such significant pruning, the plants look healthier at first, but their fruit will be weak and small and sour. A good vineyard owner is unafraid of the shears.

"Prune me gently, Lord!" one of my friends likes to say, and I echo her often. The holy and good work of God can be so painful when it is the vines of our lives and hearts that need trimming. Yet as we remain in Christ, as he himself encourages us in John 15, we, too, will face the shears.

And then we will bear the fruit.

Committed to Growth

During my chaplaincy training, I struggled mightily to get along with another woman in my cohort. I tend to be an upbeat, cheerleader type around the office (which I realize can be its own brand of irritating), while Cora[17] was the opposite. Her water glass wasn't just half empty; it was salty, too. Week after week I bit my tongue as she grumbled and complained, and then I went to my supervisory meeting and spent the entire hour grumbling and complaining about her.

"Maybe," my supervisor, Eileen, finally told me, "you need to get to know her a bit."

"I know her fine," I said. "I just don't like her." Eileen sighed.

"Be that as it may, you still have two months together, and you need to learn to work through some of this discomfort. That's your assignment for this week. Spend a little time with Cora."

I hated this assignment, but I'm not one to fail at anything if I can help it, so I planned my attack: homemade brownies, cafeteria coffee, and an invitation to take our break together the next day. Cora agreed, except she didn't drink coffee, and could we have tea instead? Sigh. Yes, of course.

As we sat on a bench in a hospital hallway and ate our treats, she began to share with me the struggles of going to seminary in her sixties, hidden health problems that made her days long and painful, a family system that taught her ministry wasn't an option because she was a woman.

"I know I come across as gruff sometimes," she said. I chuckled.

"Well, you don't have to *agree* with me!"

"Gruff is a good word for it," I responded.

Then I wagered a scary question myself. "How do *I* come across?" Cora paused. I nodded.

"It's okay," I said. "I really want to know."

"Well, you can be a little bit much sometimes," she said, looking down at the brownie in her hands. "You have this wonderful marriage and you and Daryl clearly love each other, and that's great, but it means you have a lot of support many of us don't have. Sometimes your bubbly energy feels like it's coming from someone uninterested in the pain of others. You're young and healthy, and you have your whole story ahead of you. Just ... just don't forget that not everyone is in that same boat."

The blessings of stability rush every which way, like a river of living water overflowing its banks, bringing blossoms in what was once only a desert.

"I come on a little strong, don't I?" I asked, beginning to see myself from her shoes for the very first time.

"You do," she said. "Gentleness is never a bad thing."

"Gentleness," I repeated. "Yes."

A seismic shift happened on that vinyl-padded bench in a hospital hallway smelling of disinfectant, tea, and brownies. Cora wagered honesty. I learned to begin seeing the world through her eyes, and after her, many others' too. We both made a friend. Without Eileen's prodding, I never would have ventured into such a vulnerable conversation. Knowing we had two months remaining in the program together gave me reasons to press in, but also fear of what might happen if I did. Yet attempting this tender interaction bore wonderful fruit in the vineyards of both of our lives. It often will.

The question is, Will we risk it?

● ● ●

The blessings of stability rush every which way, like a river of living water overflowing its banks, bringing blossoms in what was once only a desert. Our communities can thrive with care, commitment, and attention. So can our souls.

Still, it can be tempting to want more. What should we do when we chafe against the limitations of our place? It turns out there is grace to be found in that tension, too.

Questions for the Present

1

What kinds of work does it take
to cultivate a vineyard?

2

Read John 15:1–10. What does it look like
to abide in Jesus?

3

Where do you see God's pruning at work
in your life?

4

Why might God choose a vineyard metaphor—
with all its slow growth and potentially big harvest—
for our spiritual lives?

5

Where do you see potential harvests in your
community? Who might God be inviting you to help
with a harvest? How might you invite a friend
or a neighbor to help with yours?

PART II

The Grace of Limits

We are often so used to producing
that we forget to be present.

—RICH VILLODAS, *The Deeply Formed Life*

CHAPTER 5

Less Really Is More

The opposite of scarcity is not abundance;
the opposite of scarcity is simply enough.

—Brené Brown, *Rising Strong*

EARLY IN OUR MARRIAGE, I asked Daryl to pick up toothpaste on his way home from work. When he arrived empty handed, I assumed he'd forgotten.

"I didn't forget," he said. "I went to the store, but there were so many kinds I couldn't decide."

I held my tongue rather than mentioning the obvious—*any* toothpaste would be far superior to none. Decision fatigue had stopped him in his tracks. Overwhelmed with choices, he found himself stunned to the point of inaction in the dental care aisle at our local pharmacy. These days he pretty much only shops at Costco, where they sell only one or two options for any item, and everything in such massive quantities that we won't run out for a year. Two birds, one stone.

If you offer to bring ice cream to my party, me telling you a size, flavor, and brand is a kindness. Otherwise, I've left you to browse and wonder and make a decision without any helpful information to guide you. Chances are we will both end up a little bit frustrated. Clarity is kind. Limits are a grace. Unending options aren't the boon we sometimes believe.

In a TED Talk entitled "Choice, Happiness and Spaghetti Sauce," Malcolm Gladwell tells the story of the Prego company discovering that, while people claimed to want unlimited variety and choice, what they really wanted was either spicy, smooth, or chunky sauce. Not infinite permutations—Extra veggie! Extra chunky! Extra vodka!—but instead one of three basic types. Simplicity.

The same is true in nearly every area of our lives. We believe we want more options, limitless choice, infinite possibility, but we truly thrive within healthy, God-given limits. And here's the other surprising thing Gladwell discovered: We often don't actually even *know* what we want. "Assumption number one in the food industry used to be that the way to find out what people want to eat, what will make people happy, is to ask them," notes Gladwell. "And for all those years … no one ever said they wanted extra-chunky…. People *don't know what they want!* … A critically important step in understanding our own desires and tastes is to realize that we cannot always explain what we want deep

> **Clarity is kind.**
> **Limits are a grace.**
> **Unending options**
> **aren't the boon**
> **we sometimes**
> **believe.**

down." Gladwell goes on to share that most American adults *say* they want strong, black coffee when, in fact, the vast majority of us actually drink "milky, weak coffee."[18] Touché.

When we encounter the end of our understanding, when we don't even know what we want or why we feel the ache that we do, God is there, often with a limit we may chafe against at first. We think we want immortality when, as a quote often attributed to the actor David Niven goes, "We don't know what to do with a rainy afternoon."

Limits are a grace in so very many areas of our lives. We see this exemplified by Jesus in the Gospels. Jesus didn't closely disciple thousands, but twelve men. He rested. He regularly withdrew from the crowds to practice solitude. He ministered publicly for just a handful of years before his crucifixion, resurrection, and ascension. Paul, who wrote that he became "all things to all people," also spent significant time behind bars or under house arrest, his ministry reduced to pen and parchment that, at the time, must have felt deeply constrictive. Yet Paul's limitations have given us nearly half of the New Testament, words read by billions of people over centuries upon centuries.

Even with all our modern technology, we can still only be physically present in one location at a time. While we may project our voice or image across the world—and truly, video chatting with far-flung friends and family is one of my great joys—we ourselves are right where we are. We can chafe against this, looking continually for better opportunities or neighborhoods, different communities or school systems, greener pastures or chunkier tomato sauce, or we can begin to receive our finitude of place as the blessing which God intends it to be. There are gifts to be received as we embrace and accept our God-given limits.

"Just give me a minute!" I called from the kids' bedroom, where I was assisting our youngest in pulling up her many layers of clothing—undies, leggings, ballerina tutu. She didn't go a single place without it these days, but it made getting dressed a tricky business indeed.

"DO NOT HELP ME," she instructed sternly, holding a tiny finger up inches from my nose. "I DO IT SELF."

"Mommmmmmmm!" called the five-year-old from the living room. "I need you!"

"Mom, guess what?" asked the eight-year-old, bouncing into the room.

The toddler tipped over into a heap on the carpet and began to wail. I reached down to help her up. "NOOOOOO!" she exclaimed. "I DO IT SELF!" She cried louder.

"Mommmmmmmm!" called the five-year-old again.

"Did you know," asked the eight-year-old, raising his voice to be heard above the din, "that *racecar* is a palindrome?"

"Lincoln," I said, looking him in the eye. "I would love to hear about this *in a minute.*"

"Right," he said. "Gotcha."

"And can you see what your brother needs, please?" He scooted off to the living room.

It took several minutes of wrangling her inside-out leggings, Felicity's face screwed up in an intense glare, before she finally allowed me to assist. Girl is *tenacious.* Finally, shalom restored, I checked on the boys, who were now building a Lego city on the living room rug.

"You okay, Wils?" I asked. "What did you need?"

"Oh," he said, holding up a minifigure, "I couldn't find this guy's hat, but Lincoln helped me."

Felicity dove into the fray, and I went to the kitchen to reheat my coffee, and then to the master bedroom to check on Daryl, who was down for the count with shingles. (Yes, you can get them in your thirties. Yes, they are every bit as unpleasant as you've heard. As soon as you are old enough, *get that shot.*) He looked asleep, so I leaned over to check. His eyelids fluttered open.

"You okay, love?" I asked. He nodded. For the past week he hadn't been able to move an inch without agony. I'd started sleeping on the couch so I wouldn't accidentally cause him pain every time I rolled over in bed. My first night camping in the living room, I awoke to a family of mice skittering around behind the sofa. Apparently, we had an infestation.

"Want me to start a bath?" Daryl nodded again. "Lidocaine patch?" A third nod.

"Mommmmmm!" shouted Wilson from the living room.

"Just a minute!" I called, checking the mousetraps behind the piano on my way. A furry rump was frozen in the air. I held back a dry heave.

It was 6:42 a.m. in the midst of a global pandemic. I squared my shoulders. No reinforcements were on their way.

The Pain of the Edge

I've always prided myself on being a capable person. I'm not the smartest one in most rooms (especially rooms that include my husband, Mr. PhD Pants™. Or would that be Dr. PhD Pants™?). My common sense lacks some basic features. I'm no good with aesthetics or eyeliner or any sport involving catching and throwing, and don't even get me started on how terrifyingly inadequate I am at parallel parking. (I read somewhere that spatial reasoning is directly linked to high testosterone, and I'm going with that. I'm just *not macho enough* to parallel park.)

The one thing I have going is, like my daughter, I'm filled to the brim with tenacity. In high school I walked on a broken ankle for months. In college I ran a marathon. In graduate school I worked three jobs to help pay my way through—and then Daryl's. If trying harder were a sport, I'd go to the Olympics more than Michael Phelps.

So when the world shut down because of COVID-19, my coping mechanism kicked into high gear. I would be *so freaking capable* that our little family and our entire church of hundreds would sail through unscathed. I read all the articles, called all the doctor friends and relatives (thank you, Ian, Jill, and Judd, and also, I'm sorry), and mined the CDC and FDA and WHO and NIH websites for information. I soon realized that to keep a couple of high-risk family members as safe as possible, we'd have to pull in our borders. This had ramifications for our work and church and social lives, of course, but most pressingly it changed the trajectory of our children's education for the year. We made a decision I'd sworn on a stack of Bibles I'd never make: We decided to homeschool for one pandemic year.

My desire to never homeschool is in no way a judgment on any of you who have chosen or might choose to do it. It can be a truly wonderful, gratifying, deeply thoughtful alternative to public or private schooling. My own parents homeschooled me during junior high, and I am intensely grateful to them for pulling me out of a bullying situation during a tender developmental season. (I also know of instances where homeschooling has been a total disaster, or even used to hide abuse or neglect or provide little in the way of actual education. There are important stories to be told there, too.) I never wanted to homeschool simply because I know myself well enough to know that it isn't really my gift. I've taught for years at the college level, and I do it well in large part because college is *optional*. My students have chosen to be there (*paid* to be there!), and I don't have to spin my wheels trying to convince them why a math worksheet is worth doing in the first place.

Still, homeschooling seemed the best option for us at the time, and I was confident I could add the teacher hat to all those I already wore—mom, pastor, nurse, coach, wife, chef, nose-wiper, boo-boo kisser, Netflix monitor, author, columnist, verrrrrrry occasional laundry folder. We would be our own little family island, bubbled for a few months at a time with my parents when they were in town, but otherwise on our own to weather whatever the pandemic year might throw at us.

Of course, there was Zoom and the occasional play date from fifteen feet away, but other than that, it was all on us. On me.

● ● ●

As we began the year, I read and prepared curriculum, ordering resources, scanning textbooks, and stockpiling craft supplies. We had a toddler, a preschooler, and a second-grader. How hard could this be? The Saturday before we officially began, I planned out the activities for the week ahead—handwriting and science experiments, a world-geography card game, alphabet exercises with clothespins and paper plates, an introduction to fractions through baking, a couple Newbery Medal winners to read aloud together, and some gross-motor activities for the backyard. I stayed up past midnight on Sunday—the final day before Homeschool Fall 2020 officially commenced—getting everything *just so.*

By 10 a.m. that very first Monday, we'd worked through absolutely everything I had planned. The second-grader was in tears because I taught multiplication differently than "a real teacher"; the preschooler took one look at all the colorful manipulatives I'd set out on the dining table and told me flat out, "Yeah, I'm not doing any of that"; and the toddler had scribbled on three different walls of the house with what I prayed wasn't a permanent marker before trying to eat a handful of pony beads she found underneath the dryer.

"How'd it go?" asked Daryl, emerging from the home office at lunchtime to find the children parked in front of PBS Kids with Go-Gurts in their fists.

"This is going to be harder than I thought," I said.

The next week, I folded in some onscreen helpers—a Spanish tutor in Guatemala, a Zoom piano teacher, a good dose of Khan Academy—and it helped a little. I grew in my skill. The kids learned. God pried my hands off the last vestiges of my perfectionism, and we went full-tilt instead toward *good enough*. Day by day, we persevered that way through the entire academic year, getting curbside pickup from the library, covering the walls in butcher paper for art projects, filling the kiddie pool with water balloons for science experiments, and hiking every trail within a twenty-mile radius just to get out of the dang house for an hour or two. It was all good enough.

But here's the thing: It wasn't. Not really.

Sure, the kids did fine. Educationally, they may have even ended up a bit ahead of the curve by year's end, particularly with all the pandemic disruptions in everyone's learning. Socially, we all had stability and consistency. None of us caught COVID, or passed it on to anyone in the wider community.

But for me, every day became a painful exercise in my own finitude. I was always and only just me, even with all my education and research and skill and energy. Tenacity is no match for what we all really needed but couldn't have in any meaningful way: a larger in-person community.

"It isn't like your kids are *alone*," one friend reminded me. "They have you and Daryl, and they have each other." Indeed they did, and we got creative with socially distanced play dates, hikes with friends, FaceTime with relatives, virtual Sunday school.

The sweet sibling relationships and bonds they formed with one another are bearing good fruit to this day.

But I had never quite realized how very, very, *very* limited I am: that trying harder does not a super-human make, because none of us are super but instead only human. My reserves of good cheer and patience often ran out by lunchtime, and I resorted to hour-long walks to manage my anxiety, while Daryl worked from the home office and our pupils watched "educational television" before we resumed Lincoln's afternoon learning, Felicity's nap, and Wilson's constant fort-building.

The more I tried, the more exhausted I became, until one evening I finally found myself sobbing over a sink full of dirty dishes.

Pressed up against the barriers of my own capacity, realizing I couldn't simply sleep less or push harder or be better, I felt significant shock and dismay. I'd never *not* been able to white-knuckle my way through a season before.

Not all God's lessons are comfortable or joyful. Some are downright excruciating.

Prune me gently, Lord.

Somewhere in all of my decades of following Jesus, I'd never quite stopped believing the false gospel that I could do it all, surviving by my own wit and will and capability. Sure, I could trust God with my eternal salvation, but the rest was on me, wasn't it? I could push through! Find more capacity! TRY HARDER!

The more I tried, the more exhausted I became, until one evening I finally found myself sobbing over a sink full of dirty dishes. The week's sermon remained unfinished; the kids and I had sparred over piano practice and room tidying; my current writing project was utterly stuck; and we'd just learned that a beloved friend— our age, otherwise healthy, not yet eligible for the vaccine—had died of COVID.

"I can't do it anymore," I told Daryl. "There's nothing left in my cup. I can't pour from an empty cup!" He rubbed my shoulders. I turned for a hug. I could see weariness etched into his face, lines of haggard pandemic wrinkles, sleepless eyes, grey in his beard that wasn't there a month previous. The shingles had left a ragged scar around his torso. His shoulders carried a new heaviness upon them like a shroud. "What am I supposed to do when there's nothing left?"

"Well," he said, "I guess that's when you stop."

"How do I stop?"

"First, you let me do the dishes."

"But—"

"Court, seriously, I can do the dishes. I have a little energy for dishes." I handed over the sponge and retreated to cry in the living room.

"I am on empty," I told Jesus, curling into a blanket on the couch. "There's no more left to give." I sat in silence with God, staring out the front window, watching the neighbors head out for a walk with their dog and their stroller, waiting for some sort of divine intervention to show itself, lifting my burdens, restoring the world back to normal. Nothing came. Just more silence.

At Rest Near the Edge

I once heard a famous pastor's spouse speak about how ill-suited she was to be a pastor's wife. When her husband was installed as the pastor of a sizable city church, the ladies of the congregation met with her to tell her what was expected of her as the ministry spouse. (Let's bracket for a second the obvious problem with requiring an unpaid spouse to take on church responsibilities. As Daryl often said in the days I was ordained and he wasn't yet, "It's a lot easier to be the pastor than to be married to the pastor. One has power and a salary; the other just has expectations.") The women of the church went down the list of volunteer responsibilities the wife of the pastor was counted upon to perform: host brunches, provide hospitality for visiting preachers and missionaries, plan the annual women's tea, and so forth. The new pastor's wife balked.

"I'm not good at *any* of these things," she said.

"Well, then," one of the women said, "you will just have to do those things badly."

In times of backbreaking perfectionism, I try to remember this pastor's wife and her willingness to do things badly for the kingdom. But the more I sit with her words, the more I realize they don't go quite far enough.

Sometimes we can do things beautifully. Other times we may do them badly. But there are times for all of us that we hit our absolute limits, cry uncle, and simply need to stop. Every one of us has a breaking point. There are only so many straws a camel can carry on its back. We are simply not meant to do it all. And at the end of the day, limits are a God-given grace.

The beauty of the gospel is that God loves us so much he sent his son Jesus for us, on our behalf. And he didn't send Jesus after we'd gotten our acts together because— let's be real—we never will. Jesus came and died "while we were still sinners," as Paul writes. This beautiful, transformative God reminds us that it was never about us being *enough*. It was always and forevermore about being the beloved of God. Which we just ... *are*. Pure and simple.

This beautiful, transformative God reminds us that it was never about us being *enough*. It was always and forevermore about being the beloved of God.

We are not loved by God because of our value to society, our production capabilities, our willingness to be part of a team. We are not loved for our can-do-attitude or how we bear up under impossible circumstances. Instead, we are simply loved—loved as whole people with all of our hang-ups and glories, just as we are, right now, today. As David Benner writes in *The Gift of Being Yourself*, "The self that God persistently loves is not my prettied-up pretend self but my actual self—the real me. But, master of delusion that I am, I have trouble penetrating my web of self-deceptions and knowing this real me. I continually confuse it with some ideal self that I wish I were."[19]

The pandemic stripped away many of our coping mechanisms and regular comfort activities, leaving the delusion of our infinite capability harder to maintain. Suddenly we were just us, face-to-face with our impatience or fear of death or workaholism or selfishness. Suddenly many of us pressed up against our limits in a way we'd never done before. It turns out our ideal selves have feet of clay, and God is in the business of smashing idols.

"I can't do this anymore," I told Jesus, huddled on the couch that rainy pandemic day. I received no word from the Lord but instead a crushing sense of the physical exhaustion I'd been holding at bay. I was tired. So very, very tired. I'd minimized this weariness for months, trying to power through it. Our quarantine was a white-collar quarantine, after all. We had food and shelter and the ability to work and school from home. I wasn't saving lives by putting my own life at risk like an emergency room doctor, or even supporting the family of a frontline worker. But when we're in the thick of things, there really is no *more* or *less* hard. There's just hard.

> It's deeply, profoundly true: At the end of ourselves, there is Jesus. At the end of ourselves, we are loved.

"I guess I'll go to bed?" I prayed, more a question than a statement. It was 8:03 p.m. Hearing no divine objection, I did. As exhausted as I was, as frustrated as I was, somehow underneath the pain I could sense the faint pulse of God at work. God granted sleep, and I awoke the next morning with a teaspoon of energy refilled into my oceanic empty tank. It would be gone by breakfast, but it was a start.

● ● ●

Accepting our limits will nearly always be painful. We want to do more, be more, have more, achieve more. Yet the grace of God flows through all places, including the places we simply can't manage on our own. As Paul so wisely put it, "[The Lord] said to me, 'My grace is sufficient for you, for my power is made perfect in weakness.' Therefore I will boast all the more gladly about my weaknesses, so that Christ's power may rest on me."[20] This isn't simply a metaphor or a nice, trite saying. It's deeply, profoundly true: At the end of ourselves, there is Jesus. At the end of ourselves, we are loved.

Questions for the Present

(1)

What limits do you face today in your life?
How do they make you feel?

(2)

What is a limit you've worked to overcome?
What is one you've worked to accept?

(3)

Read 2 Corinthians 12:1–10. How might a weakness
in your life show God's power?

(4)

Are you overwhelmed or energized by unlimited
options? Why do you suppose this is so?

(5)

How can limits be a grace?

CHAPTER 6

The Miracle of Sabbath

Sabbath is not just rest from making things.
It's rest from the need to make
something of ourselves.

—Rich Villodas, *The Deeply Formed Life*

OUR YOUNGEST CHILD is a spitfire. While her older brothers napped until age five, she gave hers up soon after turning three. It wasn't that she didn't need the sleep—she did. She *really* did. The naps evaporated because she did not want to miss a moment of fun. Daryl and I would watch in exhausted amusement as she fell asleep in the car on the way home from the grocery store, in her crib while I was prepping dinner, or in the drive-thru line at In-N-Out Burger.

"What should I do?" Daryl texted me. "It's 6:05 p.m. and she just fell asleep."

"Wake her up!" I said. "Or else she'll be up all night!"

When he arrived home, Felicity had bedhead and a wild look in her eye.

"She was *out*," he said. "We tried everything to wake her. Wilson finally had to resort to tucking French fries into her mouth."

As any parent of a preschooler will tell you, kids need sleep. When they don't get enough of it, the sleep will find them—and often at inopportune times. C. S. Lewis once said that he didn't take naps after lunch; "But," he quipped, "sometimes a nap takes *me*."[21] One of our natural, biological limits is the need for sleep. According to sleep scientist William Dement, who (among other things) helped found the Stanford Center for Sleep Sciences in Medicine and has studied sleep for more than fifty years, "As far as we know, the only reason we need to sleep that is really, really solid is because we get sleepy."[22] While some of us need more than others—Daryl is perfectly happy on six hours, while I'm a roast beast with anything under eight—the fact is that God designed each of us to need a regular rhythm of waking and sleeping—work and rest. We simply can't get away from it, hard as we might wish it away.

Nowhere are we reminded more regularly of the grace of rest than in the command to honor the Sabbath. Setting aside this day for rest and worship—"praying and playing,"[23] as Eugene Peterson put it—restores us to the deep truths of the rhythms of God. We cannot continue on, full throttle, firing on all cylinders without ever stopping. We simply were not designed to function in this way. God sets us within limits for our good and for his glory, and when we begin learning to live within these limits, we will find they are grace, not burden. Writes Paul J. Pastor in his gorgeous devotional series, *The Listening Day*, "Peace is the active rest of perfect trust, the solace of surrender."[24]

God commands us to take the Sabbath, perhaps because without so stringent an imperative, we would ignore it even more than we do. Even with the knowledge that it sits in a list of "Thou Shalts" along with worshiping God alone, honoring our parents, and keeping the Lord's name holy, we tend to treat it as optional at best. We are too important to take a break, we tell ourselves. Our work is too vital, our needs too great.

God designed each of us to need a regular rhythm of waking and sleeping— work and rest. We simply can't get away from it.

Beyond our inner impulse to keep going and going and going, Energizer Bunnies all, there is the external reality that many of us have work or school schedules that don't easily allow for a weekly Sabbath. As a pastor, my church expects me to work Sundays (the nerve!). Sunday can be one of the busiest days of the week for those in the service or hospitality industries. I know more than a handful of folks who would love to take a day to rest, but that would be choosing between rent and food, or prescription medications and the electric bill. Part of the ache of our modern world is that our economic systems don't often recognize rest as a common good, or fair wages—including essentials like health care and paid sick leave—as a biblical imperative.

The Old Testament speaks not only of the personal command to Sabbath but also to the cultural, social command. The Sabbath is for people, yes, but it's also for the culture as a whole, for the farmland, and for the beasts of burden. Exodus 23 describes it this way:

> For six years you are to sow your fields and harvest the crops, but during the seventh year let the land lie unplowed and unused. Then the poor among your people may get food from it, and the wild animals may eat what is left. Do the same with your vineyard and your olive grove.
>
> Six days do your work, but on the seventh day do not work, so that your ox and your donkey may rest, and so that the slave born in your household and the foreigner living among you may be refreshed.
>
> Be careful to do everything I have said to you. Do not invoke the names of other gods; do not let them be heard on your lips.[25]

In other words, Exodus 23 ties breaking Sabbath to idolatry. When we begin ignoring God's command to rest (and fail to let our friends and pastors and plow horses and fields rest as well), it is often a sign of deeper disobedience at work. Where the Sabbath is not kept holy, you can be sure people have begun to turn away from God.

This is a sobering truth for us all, and perhaps even more so for those of us in ministry, where we often hear boasting of working weeks upon end without a break. At best, many pastors often offer tongue-in-cheek sermons on Sabbath practices while admitting they don't hold to those biblical lines very well themselves. While I'm all for healthy self-disclosure from the pulpit and admitting that none of us is without sin, something is amiss when those working for God humblebrag about working in ways God never intended. We must never make light of a command.

Yet sometimes, when ministry professionals overfunction, there is a more systemic issue at work. Even pastors, directors, elders, and lay leaders dedicated to healthy Sabbath practices will have a serious uphill battle if the rest of the church leadership—and much of the laity—isn't on board. Workaholic cultures demand faith leaders made in their own image, and the cost of this unhealth is steep for all. Recovering the Sabbath is a communal act, and while pastors can help lead the charge, the line will be nearly impossible to hold alone.

When I pastored in rural Wisconsin, I'd often drive out of town on my Sabbath because it was so hard to say no to the people I loved if I saw them face-to-face. (It didn't help that we lived thirty feet from the church on the main street in a small town. Work and home life were tricky to separate!) A ten-minute conversation in line at the grocery store often turned into an invitation to coffee or dinner, which often turned into an impromptu brainstorming session about Sunday school or the upcoming town festival or how we could better empower our youth as they prepared for their mission trip. All good things, but not on the Sabbath, where unplugging from tasks is essential. After bumbling over my "No, thank you, not today" a time too many, I finally realized it was easier to take my Bible and journal and drive away for a bit. After all, my Sabbath day was Friday and theirs was Sunday—it wasn't their job to protect *my* Sabbath. But it *was* mutually our calling to help each other live into God's gift of rest.

Taking the Day

Sabbath aids us in our quest to practice presence, giving us time and space to listen, feel, reflect, and rest. This can be painful—not everything feels good, leaving work undone is uncomfortable, and opening our hearts to the Lord is vulnerable indeed—but it is ultimately a gift and grace. As a yoga instructor once told me, "In order to heal, you need to feel." The Sabbath puts us in touch with our nerve endings once again.

Feeling our feelings can be a dicey proposition. Many a pastor returns from their sabbatical—an extended Sabbath of a month or two, given to ministers after seven years or so in the pastorate—reenergized for the work ahead, but perhaps just as many return having discovered that they are ready to move on to another church or even leave ministry entirely. In fact, my own denominational guidelines now encourage a pastor to commit to staying at a church for at least six months following a sabbatical: a new suggestion written in part to stem the tide of pastors who didn't know they were burned out until they had a few moments of peace and quiet in which to

> **Sabbath aids us in our quest to practice presence, giving us time and space to listen, feel, reflect, and rest.**

think about it. I'd wager that most of those pastors didn't have a regular, healthy Sabbath practice, for it is in these repeated, weekly spaces and silences that we remember the ministry for what it is—ultimately the work of God, of which we are merely shepherds. It also helps us see us for what we are—frail vessels given the sacred responsibility to walk alongside the people of God in a particular time and place. We aren't their Savior; Jesus has already done that bit. What freedom and relief. What rest.

The weekly rhythmic grace of Sabbath reorients us to the cosmic nature of time, held securely in the hands of God.

Sabbath also reminds us that all time belongs to the Lord. God has numbered our days, as the psalmist says; we can trust that we have enough time for what God intends for us. It is all too easy to fluctuate between frenetic activity (there is not enough time!) and boredom (what should I do with all this time?). The weekly rhythmic grace of Sabbath reorients us to the cosmic nature of time, held securely in the hands of God. We have the time that we need; no more, no less. As Howard Thurman notes, "I cannot wait to begin living meaningfully when I have more time, because all the time that I can ever experience is the time interval of my moment."[26] Opening space to enjoy Sabbath rest with God amidst our busy lives may feel a bit unsettling when we begin; there will be a natural "hangover" of sorts from our constant running to and fro. But it is in these open spaces that we can begin to rediscover the presence of God, both within ourselves and externally—through Scripture, our circumstances, and our neighbors.

A Simple Beginning

If you aren't sure where to begin, here is a simple "how to" I often offer to those asking for a starting place.

First, schedule the Sabbath. If possible, it should be weekly and repeatable, both because this lessens the burden of having to keep track of it and because this will naturally begin to set your soul's rhythm. If your schedule is erratic, it may not be possible to celebrate the Sabbath at the same time each week, but don't confuse things you have to do with things you simply *want* to do. (For example, you may *have to* work, but you may simply *want to* join a softball league that meets Sunday mornings. The latter might be set aside to respond to God's call and command to a weekly Sabbath.)

> Dedicate your Sabbath to the threefold practices of worship, rest, and play.

Block off the calendar and keep it dedicated. Then, when you're tempted to overschedule or put optional work or social obligations on the docket, you'll have a visual reminder of what you intend to do. If you don't keep a calendar, you may want to work even more intentionally to set aside the same time each and every week so it doesn't get swallowed up inadvertently.

Secondly, take the time. It really is as simple as that! Dedicate your Sabbath to the threefold practices of worship, rest, and play. Stay off your email (and indeed, all screens as much as possible). Pause your social media. As your mind and soul begin to rest, you'll often feel out of sorts and cranky at first. This is normal! Expected, even. Barbara Brown Taylor calls it "Sabbath sickness."[27] It will pass. Go for a walk, exercise, grab a novel, drive to church, open your Bible, light a fire, set up a board game, take a nap, write in your journal. Slowly the gifts of Sabbath will begin to make themselves known.

We do not often live present to ourselves or to the Lord. It is a new skill to learn, and one we will need repeated practice in. Be patient with yourself. Get used to saying, "I can make a note of that, but I won't do it today." Resist the urge to make just one work call or send just one email, and in doing so, open yourself back up to the frenetic pace of the regular workweek. Breathe deeply. The feelings of stress and overwhelm will pass, and often you will find God's peace right underneath them. It's been on offer to you all the time.

The act of rest is itself a radical witness to the good God we serve, a reminder to all that we are more than what we do or produce or achieve.

Finally, give thanks to God for the Sabbath gift. As you close the time, remember the lessons of rest, play, and worship—God's weekly reminders to each of us that we are, as Henri Nouwen so often put it, the Beloved.

That's it! It's so simple a child can practice it and, like all things worth learning, so challenging we will spend our entire lives mining its depths and yet never get to the bottom of it all. God's goodness knows no floor or ceiling.

● ● ●

The study of Sabbath has seen a resurgence lately, and I'm so grateful for it. Still, it will be forever countercultural to set down our tools, leave work undone, and sit quietly in the presence of the Lord. The act of rest is itself a radical witness to the good God we serve, a reminder to all that we are more than what we do or produce or achieve, and that it is the deep rhythms of God that sustain us and our world—not our striving.

I'm still learning. As a recovering achievement addict, I sometimes find myself twitching in my chair on the Sabbath, eager to spring from it to just send one ... more ... email. Old habits die hard, but God is gently persistent and oh, so faithful.

The grace of limits has its beginning and ending in God's Sabbath gift. Here we find our rest and hope. Here we pause long enough to listen to the beat of our own heart, and underneath that faithful rhythm, the deeper, stronger pulse of the Holy Spirit holding us all in love.

Questions for the Present

(1)

When you hear the word *Sabbath*, what do you think and feel? What associations do you have with it?

(2)

Read Exodus 23:10–13. How is the Sabbath command designed to affect individuals? Communities?

(3)

Have you ever taken a regular Sabbath?
What was it like?

(4)

In what ways might God meet us in our regular Sabbath practice?

(5)

How might you accept God's Sabbath command in a deeper way this week? This month?
On a regular basis?

CHAPTER 7

The Scandal of Particularity

We are looking forward to the only One
in whom the promise of peace
will some day be fulfilled.

—Fleming Rutledge, *Advent*

I *KNOW NOT TO* read the news before bed. We all know not to do this, don't we?

I *know* not to read the news before bed, which is why Daryl sometimes discovers me crouched under our down comforter clutching my phone, a quivering mass of anxiety and insomnia.

"You okay?" he'll ask.

"I'm worried," I'll say.

"About what?"

It might be anything, really: inflation, school shootings, climate change, Chechnya, viruses, toxic algae, the possible cancellation of *Survivor*. Truly, there is much to fear.

I've tried taking Paul's instructions not to be anxious but "instead pray"[28] to heart, but I'll be honest: Even praying my way through the ills of the planet and its people is too much for me some days. Paul's original audience wasn't concerned with happenings in the Western hemisphere, after all, or even far beyond their own limited borders. They didn't know about permafrost. They couldn't log on to Facebook.

But here we sit, with unlimited doom-scrolling potential at our fingertips, and some days we just can't stop. The world is a mess. Our neighborhoods are a mess. Our hearts are a mess. The crushing, horrifying weight of the sins and savageries of the world press down upon us until we can scarcely breathe.

We simply aren't designed to bear such weight.

God sets each of us among a particular group of people in a particular place for a particular season for a *reason*. We aren't called to bear the sins of the world—there is One who already did this, and he is the only one who can. Instead, God invites us to care in particular—right here, right now. John 3:16 tells us that God so loved the world, but nowhere are we commanded to do the same. We are invited instead to love the world through our specific corner of it: "Love your neighbor as yourself," God chisels into Moses's stone tablets.[29] We are to love from where we are.

As St. Augustine wrote, "Since you cannot do good to all, you are to pay special attention to those who, by accidents of time, or place, or circumstances, are brought into closer connection with you."[30] "The earth is the LORD's, and everything in it."[31] We are not given this entire great and terrible burden to hold, and if we take it upon ourselves, we may find ourselves crushed by a weight we were never intended to bear.

Instead, we are invited to accept the grace of limits—acquiescing to our particular place and time and people. After all, even just loving those God sets before us is quite a steep task indeed. One of the first discoveries we make in entering into community of any kind is that people are difficult. We're complicated. We're messy. We come with lots of hang-ups and preferences and foibles. Sometimes we may try to take on to the burdens of the world because those are huge and general and *out there* rather than attending to the smaller—yet often more difficult—task of loving the neighbor right in front of us. Millions of people are starving this very moment in a far-off land, and hundreds more in a town nearby, but if perseverating about their plight keeps us from cooking dinner for our next-door neighbor in need, well, we may have missed the boat on Christ's call to love that very particular person, right here, right now, as ourselves.

A Particular God

The myth of our time is that endless possibility is a good thing. It rarely, if ever, is. We are finite creatures set in a world of limitations because of God's love for us. As Daryl once put it—not in his dissertation but in a tweet, because occasionally that is where true profundity shows itself—"Only God is good in general [...] because God's goodness includes every particular goodness. Every other thing is good precisely because of [its] particularity."[32] This principle extends across disciplines, from our relationships to our land. As Fleming Rutledge once prayed, following Hurricane Ida and all the destruction it wrought, "O Lord our God, creator of this beautiful planet and savior of all humankind, look mercifully upon us now in grave danger as a result of our heedlessness ... grant that we may once again live within the boundaries you have created, for our good and for your great glory."[33] Boundaries, limitations, finitude— these are part of God's created order, graces, and goods designed for our flourishing. Will we acquiesce to living within them, or will we ignore them or fight against them—and then suffer the consequences as a result?

The myth of our time is that endless possibility is a good thing. It rarely, if ever, is.

The theological arc to this idea is that one of the persons of the Trinity comes to us in the same way—as a person with actual arms and legs and a beating heart and a sweaty brow. Theologians have a phrase for the idea: They call it the scandal of particularity. It's the bizarre truth that Jesus Christ saves the world, though he is only one particular person who lived in a particular place and time. (And now lives eternally, of course.)

The incarnation reminds us that we can't know or love things in general but only by knowing them specifically. Indeed, this is the only way we ourselves are loved. For example, I might enjoy the *idea* of children, but my love only becomes real in the presence of an individual child—perhaps my new baby niece, as I look into her deep blue eyes, touch her downy head, examine her impossibly tiny fingers. This baby is not all babies; she is Pippa Noel.

Richard Rohr writes, "Love—God incarnate—always begins with particulars: this woman, this dog, this beetle, this Moses, this Virgin Mary, this Jesus of Nazareth. It is the individual and the concrete that opens the heart ... Without it there is no true devotion or faith, but only argumentative theories."[34] Many a person claims to love humanity "in general" but can't be bothered to check on an ailing relative, speak kindly to a barista, or make space for another driver to merge during a traffic jam. It is only in the individual moments with actual, live people that our faith and love come to fruition. Annie Dillard puts it this way: "The 'scandal of particularity' is the only world that I, in particular, know."[35]

> It's only by making distinct commitments to people and places that we are able to grow deep roots.

This scandal applies to place as well. For all the hours we spend on Zoom or FaceTime or social media, we cannot hold and touch those friends unless we get up and go to where they are. Choosing a place is also *not* choosing near-infinite other places we might adopt as our own. It's one reason it took Daryl a good long while to propose.

"I love you," he told me more than once, "I'm just not totally sure I want to close down every other possibility." It wasn't that he was looking over my shoulder at other women (God help him—I wouldn't have stood by for any of *that*); he just wasn't certain God was calling him to marriage at the tender age of twenty-four. (Honestly, we were basically infants when I walked down the aisle. There should have been a law.) Yet it's only by making distinct commitments to people and places that we are able to grow deep roots. Our marriage now wears the grace of sixteen years of nurture and tenderness and hard conversations and kindnesses and listening and counseling and late-night chats over ice cream and popcorn. Committing to one another changed us and continues to shape us, much like settling into a particular place will, if we let it. If we attempt to be everywhere and leave all options open, in the long run we will find ourselves placeless and people-less. It is by rooting to our place, right here in the present, that we step into the journey of maturity and flourishing.

The Grass Is Just Green

Driving home from the beach, Daryl sighed and pointed toward my passenger window. I looked out to see a huge plume of smoke rising over the mountains to the east.

"Any chance that's just a house fire?" I asked.

"I don't think so."

I bit my tongue so as not to let a choice word fly in front of our sandy, soggy children chattering happily from the back seat. To say fire season stresses me out would be like saying Mike Tyson has a tiny face tattoo. I grew up in the wooded-but-wet forests of northern Wisconsin. Fires weren't unheard of, but they were very, very rare. Today in California dozens of fires commonly burn at one time, some of them thousands upon thousands of acres. Many are to the north or east of us; seldom do we get any right at our back door. Poor Daryl regularly tries to explain to me that urban areas don't burn well, that it's the foothills and the mountains and the canyons that take the brunt of fire season.

"That's probably true," I tell him, believing none of it, "but remember the Chicago fire. The Peshtigo fire. Those were *urban*."

"In the 1800s," he reminds me. *"When buildings were all made of wood."*

"Like our *house*," I tell him. That's when one of us usually heads out for a walk muttering about Mrs. O'Leary's cow (me) or urban density (him).

Though I'll admit that our particular neighborhood is unlikely to burn (not impossible, mind you, but unlikely), the air quality alone once forced us to evacuate. Waking to ash raining on our car, our lawn, and our driveway was unsettling, to say the least. California would be heaven if it weren't for the fires. And the cost of living. And the lack of Culver's restaurants. And ... well, you get the point. Every single place has its opportunities for discontent, even one as sunny and citrusy as California.

> God calls us to love the ones right in front of us, impossible as that might seem.

The truth is that committing to a particular place is never easy on this side of eternity. Not only does the drumbeat of bigger and better pound consistently, but as soon as we plug into our communities, our churches, and our neighborhoods, we will inevitably realize that the people we live near aren't saints. They're sinners, just like we are. The temptation then is to detach, unplug, and look for a better place with better people. The bad news is that there aren't any. Sure, there might be communities where we fit in more easily or our neighbors won't play trash can drums at 1 a.m., or we will meet people who speak our native language, or share our values, or root for the correct sports teams (Wisconsin Badgers for LYFE!). Still, no matter where we land, we will face the difficulty of existing around other human beings. And God calls us to love the ones right in front of us, impossible as that might seem.

In *Life Together*, Dietrich Bonhoeffer describes the difficulty this way: "Without Christ we should not know God, we could not call upon Him, nor come to Him. But, without Christ we also would not know our brother, nor could we come to him. The way is blocked by our own ego. Christ opened up the way to God and to our brother."[36] Indeed, it is only through Jesus that we have hope of finding contentment in local community, whether it be our imperfect neighborhoods, our local churches, or even our friend circles.

Even Moses Struggled

By Numbers 11, God's people have seen incredible glory. The Israelites marched through the Red Sea on dry ground. They drank water from a rock in the desert. They ate bread that fell from heaven. God's presence went before them in a pillar of cloud or fire to guide them. Their sandals—no longer under warranty after hundreds of miles of wandering—never even wore out!

And yet.

The human capacity to complain knows no bounds. There, safe in the wilderness, no longer slaves to a cruel Pharaoh, they realize they haven't had a burger in a while. How dare God be so cruel? Cue the whining. Cue the whimpering. Cue the grumbling and complaining and kvetching and sarcasm.

Cue also Moses realizing he is *over it.*

"I cannot carry all these people by myself; the burden is too heavy for me," he tells the Lord. "If this is how you are going to treat me, please go ahead and kill me."[37] This attitude isn't even an isolated incident in Scripture. Elijah and Jonah both have similar moments, too.[38]

As a beloved seminary professor of mine used to say when students told him they were headed into the ministry because they "liked people": *Have you MET people?*

Even the Lord is angry with the grumbling Israelites in Numbers 11. Before Moses makes his impassioned plea, the Lord becomes "exceedingly angry."[39] It is not wrong to grow weary with difficult people.

It is in the particularities of place and people that we are tested and tried, encouraged and uplifted, frustrated and freed.

Moses begs for relief—even if it comes through death—but God responds by surrounding him with ... wait for it ... *more people.*

The people are the problem—grumblers all—and the people are the solution, too. God tells Moses to bring him seventy leaders.

"They will share the burden of the people with you so you will not have to carry it alone," says the Lord.[40] When the going gets tough, often our impulse is to isolate. Yet God draws us out and together for our own good. It is in the particularities of place and people that we are tested and tried, encouraged and uplifted, frustrated and freed.

It's true for me, right here where I am.

It's true for you, right where you are, too.

Questions for the Present

1

What is one particular thing you love about where you live? One thing you dislike?

2

What is one particular thing you love about the people who live near you? What is one thing you dislike about them?

3

Read Numbers 11:4–15. What is frustrating Moses? What does he ask God to do for him?

4

When have you been so frustrated with your place or people that you were tempted to throw in the towel? What happened?

5

Read Numbers 11:16–17. How does it transform Moses's burden to have it shared? How might God be inviting you to share your particular burdens within your community?

CHAPTER 8

The Mercies of Enough

I hate waiting.

—Inigo Montoya, *The Princess Bride*

Back when I was searching for my first pastoral call, I quickly became frustrated with a lack of options in my area. Unless I wanted to commute multiple hours each way, there were no churches in my denomination looking for a newly minted pastor. Now that I've served in ministry for over a decade, I get it: New pastors are a gamble indeed. Untried and untested, I was all enthusiasm without experience, a puppy begging to pull a sled for the Iditarod.

I shouldn't say there were *no* jobs, because there was one. It was part-time, ten hours per week, and it had been vacant for half a decade.

This is what we in ministry call *a red flag*.

Certain churches don't want a pastor as much as a punching bag. Most don't mean to undermine the leaders they call to serve them, but entrenched habits die hard, and change is unsettling. It is nearly always easier to take down a scapegoat than to take a hard look inside. I'd learned in seminary to go in to any interview with my eyes wide open for deep-seated signs of unhealth like these. This church wasn't for me, especially not so early on in my formation. But there was one line in their ministry form that I still think about from time to time over a decade later: "You'll need to be patient," it said, "because change comes slowly here."

Our limits can help us learn patience, or they can break us down in frustration as we rail against them. Often it's both.

I admired the honesty of this church. Surely they had stories to tell. Perhaps previous pastors had come in determined to lead change and had instead been outlasted by folks who knew they'd remain long after any newbies burned out. Maybe the church had suffered a trauma—a bad, too-fast or wrongheaded change that they were still reeling from half a decade since. Whatever the reason, their plea for patience was rich with wisdom. Indeed, change comes slowly. In most instances, this is how God designed change to occur.

One Step. Then Another.

Patience is a virtue. Scripture itself says so, the apostle Paul labeling it a fruit of the Spirit. Our limits can help us learn patience, or they can break us down in frustration as we rail against them. Often it's both, for the path toward patience is a rocky one indeed.

I was reminded of a tongue-in-cheek prayer during a recent encounter with laryngitis: "Lord, give me patience, and give it to me now!" One of my most valuable vocational tools is my voice. As a parent, a speaker, and a pastor, I spend a lot of time talking, whether reading a bedtime story, teaching a class, or standing in a pulpit. At least, that's my usual. But then I started losing my voice. At first, it'd grow patchy over a period of hours, and then it would drop out entirely, leaving me with only a hoarse—and sometimes painful—whisper. I saw my general practitioner, who said I'd likely strained it from overuse and should rest it until it came back. So I did. But it didn't come back within a day or two, or even a week.

So I rested my voice, one day at a time, for three weeks. Three long weeks of parenting-by-charades, canceling speaking engagements, and pastoring largely by email. My parents visited from Wisconsin, and we spent an entire day silently standing in Legoland lines, with the kids filling in the blanks for me when I couldn't get by with hand gestures. I whispered my way through meetings. I waved and smiled at the neighbors by the mailbox, and then, when they asked me questions, waved and smiled awkwardly some more before retreating to the house to grab my phone and text an explanation.

By month's end, my voice had returned, raspy but present. Relief. Rejoicing. The first morning I could sing in the shower, I cried. Daryl and I assumed the status quo was back and the laryngitis was a blip, so I returned to my normal routine. I preached, read bedtime stories, and hosted a beloved friend from out of town. Never mind that I was eating cough drops like candy, drinking gallons of water, and still running out of voice by day's end. I had *something*, and I was grateful. Then, standing in our kitchen, preparing for Daryl's fortieth birthday party, a backyard gathering with friends and food, I asked one of the children to help with a chore, and it started failing again.

"Daryl!" I croaked in a panic, "it's happening again!"

By mid-party, my voice was gone completely. A friend stepped in to run the birthday trivia, and I fought back despair.

Cue the familiar, hated dance again. Whistles and whiteboards, texting and emails, frustrated rounds of guess-what-Mommy-is-trying-to-say with the children. Then multiple doctors and a specialist and a vocal cord scope; and, finally, a definitive diagnosis. The issue was likely a solvable one, praise be, but only with major lifestyle changes, medications, and multiple weeks— or perhaps more—of complete rest.

"It's pretty bad," the specialist told me. "There's risk of permanent damage without proper recovery time. Take the meds, follow my instructions, and I'll take another look in three weeks"

I sat in my car in the med center parking lot and texted Daryl.

"I'll be home in a bit," I said. "First I need to have a good cry."

I tried to channel my 12 percent British heritage and keep a stiff upper lip. I tried to be creative and pivot. (Am I the only one who's developed a serious eye twitch whenever I hear that word?) I tried to communicate in other ways, downloading a text-to-speech app that made me sound like a female Stephen Hawking and caused our youngest to believe "the robot" knew her name. Each of these things helped a little bit, but all fell far short of the one thing I so desperately wanted: my voice.

● ● ●

I'm an Enneagram 3 (for any of you who read *Uncluttered*, I once believed I was a 2, but I've since discovered differently!), and E3s are allllll about achievement. We accomplish things. We get things done. We churn out the work and don't blink at an extra project or two. If we tell you we'll have the results in your hands by 5 p.m., you'd better believe you'll have it by 4:45, just in case you need anything more from us before the day is done. Beyoncé is believed to be an Enneagram 3, if that tells you anything. So is Leslie Knope. One of my mentor pastors once called me a thoroughbred.

"You like to go *fast*," he told me.

"Yes, I do!" I beamed.

"That ... that isn't always *good*, Courtney," he said. *Lies!*

Yet life comes for us all, and the kindness of God means most of us will have the opportunity to grow spiritually by facing down our demons, one way or another. All of life is a school for holiness.

This loss of my voice didn't just stink; it made me question my purpose. What is a pastor without her voice? A parent who cannot sing a bedtime song, ask a question, or explain a new concept? How can a person be a friend solely over text? I felt helpless as a kitten—and as out of control as a kitten in a typhoon. To make matters worse, my timeline for healing was open-ended. Hopefully the medication would work and my voice would return in its fullness. But we wouldn't know for weeks. In the meantime, I could do nothing but wait and perseverate and pray.

All of life is a school for holiness.

A Voice for the Voiceless

Late on Saturday after Daryl's party, he scrambled to rewrite my sermon for his own voice. The next morning, he preached the lights out, and I held myself together, mouthing the words to all the songs so I could participate in part, listening and taking notes on my own sermon to give my hands something to do, sporting my homemade name tag with the words LOST MY VOICE scrawled in Sharpie: a little wearable sign I could point to when the inevitable post-worship questions came.

As the service ended, people began filtering out. A teenager asked if she could pick up our kids from class, and I gave her a thumbs-up. I stood gathering my things when I noticed one of our prayer ministers standing alone. I put down my papers and walked over to her.

She put a hand on my shoulder and looked into my eyes.

"Your voice?" she asked. I nodded. She asked God for comfort and healing, for reminders of his presence and provision and care. I stood there with her underneath the beautiful wooden cross at the front of the worship space, the cross underneath which I stood to preach, to baptize, and now, to come vulnerably before God asking for mercy.

"And Lord, when she cannot speak, I ask that you would be her voice." A shimmer of tears blurred my vision as she spoke amen, and I silently slipped over to the closet behind the cross to weep and breathe and gather myself. Over the frustrating weeks that followed, her prayer became knit into my heart. Much of my prayer up until that point in my life had been to be a faithful voice for God to my children, my community, my congregation. Now I was praying the inverse.

Lord, be my voice.

● ● ●

The suffering of turning my personality inside out, opening my hands to the grace of limits, learning the bitterest virtue for an Enneagram 3—the virtue of humility—was painful. It opened up a whole host of questions: Who was I if I couldn't speak? Why was God allowing this to happen? Was I capable of being faithful in the small things, or had I become so accustomed to speeding past them on the way toward bigger and better that I'd simply implode with the effort?

If life teaches us nothing else, it will teach us humility. I couldn't push any harder or faster or farther, so little by little I began to stop. I slowly began to realize my true place in the universe—not as a driver but as a passenger. The gift of weakness is a mirror allowing us to see ourselves as the size we really are—no longer looming large with pride or small with false humility, but the actual size of our selves: fitted to nestle perfectly in the arms of a tremendously big God.

Little by little, my comfort arrived, but not in the ways I'd imagined. I hoped for quick healing but instead received more uncertainty and waiting. I'd waited for spiritual feelies, but God answered this prayer most often through other people: The prayer minister. Daryl jumping in with my sermon. A pastor and friend leading my preaching retreat, speaking from my own notes as though they were her own, and refusing to let me split the fee. "They're your words, Courtney," she said. "I'm just your voice."

But God surprised me with strangers, too. Over and over again, people were remarkably, ridiculously kind. A pharmacist went out of his way, with a flurry of text messages from me, to get a difficult prescription rushed. A fast-food cashier ran to the back to grab a pen and paper when my menu-pointing attempts were unsuccessful.

The prayer was being answered in real time through the people of God and people I'd never met. I was humbled and awed and felt my eyes opening to a new and abundant grace.

It wasn't what I'd wanted.

It wasn't what I'd asked for.

But perhaps it would be just enough.

Questions for the Present

1

Where do you face change in your life today?
How does it feel?

2

What is hardest for you when it comes to
navigating change?

3

What limits in your life have you chosen?
Which haven't you? Do they feel different?

4

Read Proverbs 22:4. How is humility connected
to fearing God? To riches? What kinds of riches
do you think the author means?

5

When have you experienced God meeting
your needs with enough?

PART III

The Joy of Presence

I go down to the water to cool my eyes.

—ANNIE DILLARD, *Pilgrim at Tinker Creek*

CHAPTER 9

Know Your Place

Paris was all so ... Parisian. I was captivated by the wonderful wrongness of it all—the unfamiliar fonts, the brand names in the supermarket, the dimensions of the bricks and paving stones. Children, really quite small children, speaking fluent French!

—David Nicholls, *Us*

DARYL AND I took the highway north, frozen prairie grasses waving brittlely by the roadside, the sky growing early winter-dark. I glanced at him out of the corner of my eye. Twenty-two and tall, with broad shoulders, his shaved head covered by a knit cap.

My phone beeped. It was a text from my mom.

There's a snowstorm on its way. Are you still driving to that concert?

"Who's that?" Daryl asked.

"My mom," I said. "She's worried about the weather."

"Are you?" he asked. He was a child of California, and even after four years at our shared Chicagoland college, weather of any kind made him nervous. For me, a girl born and bred in the frozen north, anything short of a tornado warning warranted no more than a shrug. Weather was the stuff of small talk, not wasted concert tickets.

"Nah," I said. I truly wasn't worried, but even if I had been, a blizzard wrapped inside a hurricane wouldn't have been enough to keep me from this concert. It wasn't the prospect of seeing music performed live (Jason Mraz was fabulous, but I'm short, so mostly I see shoulders when I go to standing-room-only concerts); it was the opportunity to spend hours in the car with Daryl.

Daryl, my dear friend for nearly four years whom I'd suddenly started to notice in a new way. He wasn't just another boy from class anymore. I'd watched him grow up into wisdom. Gravitas. Depth. Plus, there were those broad, sexy shoulders. The only ones I actually *wanted* to look at.

Daryl first asked me on a date four years earlier, and I'd said no. To be fair, he asked me over our computer network's Instant Messenger, which wasn't super suave, but also he was *way* too serious for me. He literally told people he wanted to be an evangelist like Billy Graham. While that might be noble, I really didn't want to date an evangelist. Too much pressure. Also, I was pretty sure evangelists would be bad kissers.

Now, twenty-two years old and wearing my fanciest peach-colored t-shirt from Old Navy and a faux suede jacket I thought made me look literary, I was hoping he would be brave enough to ask me again, four years after his opening salvo.

In the years between, I'd dated a string of Bad News Boys™ whom we need not mention (except to say that David, if you're reading this, I hope you finally met someone you love more than video games). Daryl dated a bit, too, including a British girl he met in an Oxford library who was, it turned out, more interested in marrying a nobleman than a California kid. The British class system is *wild*.

Daryl eventually dropped his stadium-filling Billy Graham aspirations in lieu of studying theology, and now here we were, both single, driving together to Milwaukee. I hoped this concert would serve as a catalyst and that maybe, just maybe, he'd risk asking me to date him once again. I couldn't ask him, of course, because I was well-schooled in the evangelical subculture of Girls Don't Do That.

So I waited. And hoped. And braved the blizzard. Snowstorm, shmostorm. Parents overreact about potential danger all the time. Plus, the farmland all around us was frozen but bare, and stars were just beginning to wink overhead. The night was clear.

Three hours later, we emerged from the Eagle Ballroom into downtown Milwaukee. At least, I thought it was still Milwaukee. I couldn't tell for certain, since an entire universe of powder had emptied into the streets. It looked like Hoth. We could barely trudge to the car in our sneakers, and when we finally located it in a sea of curbside white mounds, the snow had risen to its bumper, with buckets more raining down upon us.

We brushed the car off with our sleeves and his scarf, and then I got inside to start the engine, hoping for a miracle. It turned over, but then so did our wheels, spinning out over and over again in a futile attempt to get any traction on the slippery street.

"Can you push?" I yelled out the cracked window. He slipped over to the back and laid his hands on the trunk.

"Tell me when!" he called out. He pushed and I hit the accelerator again. Nothing but a spray of slush slung from beneath our tires. Daryl trudged back to the window, his sweater coated in snow, his sneakers soaked.

"Now what?" he said. I bit my lip. *Now what* indeed.

Just then, a handful of people emerged from the house across the sidewalk. I blushed—we'd been yelling at the top of our lungs, and the evening was late.

"Looks like you need a hand!" one of the guys called, pulling on a jacket. "Hold on." He retreated down the alley, followed by the three others.

"What are they doing?" Daryl asked.

"Maybe getting sand?" I said.

"Sand?"

"Or a shovel."

Soon three people surrounded our trunk, bending to check the wheels and sprinkling kitty litter under our tires. They told Daryl to get in the passenger side as the first guy came back with a wide-blade shovel. He dug out our front wheels and then shoveled a path to the street.

"You're still a little stuck," he said. "We're going to rock the car. Sit tight."

"What—" Daryl started again.

"This is good," I said. "Now *shhhhh*. I need to pay attention." They rocked, I revved, and at last the tires found purchase. We fishtailed into the street. Our pit crew cheered.

"What now?" Daryl asked.

"Now we drive back to school," I said.

"But what about them?" he asked. "Do we pay them?"

I laughed. "Pay them? Of course not."

"But they helped us."

"Wasn't that nice?"

"Why did they help us?"

"Because we needed help. We'd do the same for them." I gripped the steering wheel more tightly. Driving through this much powder was going to be a trip.

"We would?" he asked.

"California, meet Wisconsin."

Where are you from? To some of us, that question—so popular during my college orientation—is simple. I grew up in Eagle River, Wisconsin, a resort town of 1,344 people nestled in the pine forests of the northern Midwest. Daryl hails from Burbank, a studio city outside Los Angeles, filled with classic diners, scrubby hillsides, and ethereal celebrities. My children call Southern California home, and are thus convinced that 60° qualifies as "cold." (Try telling that to my sisters' children, growing up in Minnesota.)

One thing is certain: Place matters. It shapes us. It speaks to us.

For others, the question of origin is much more complicated—as us first-years quickly discovered, all those years ago. Perhaps you moved every few years as a child, or you were born in one country but emigrated to another. Our relationships with place can be nostalgic and joyful, complicated and traumatic, stable and secure, or all of the above. One thing is certain: Place matters. It shapes us. It speaks to us. The culture of location seeps into our psyches in ways we don't always understand—until we're being shoved out of a snowbank by strangers.

●　●　●

"That would never happen in Los Angeles," Daryl told me as we crept our way toward the highway. A highway I prayed would be well-plowed.

"It doesn't snow in Los Angeles," I said.

"Yeah, but in L.A. if people come out of their houses it isn't to help you."

"That's because it doesn't snow."

"But even if it did—"

"If it snowed in Los Angeles regularly, people would help each other. In cold climates you know that it'll be you stuck in that snowbank next time and you'll be the one needing help. Plus, not helping someone in freezing weather can potentially be fatal."

"Huh."

Two years later, I married that California boy. Today, with sixteen years of marriage under our belts, and despite our many similarities—both white, both nerds, both raised evangelical on a steady diet of Awana and *Adventures in Odyssey*—we still occasionally find ourselves shocked by each other's cultural differences. For example, he believes that a Green Bay Packers hoodie is "not appropriate to wear to church."

Whatevs.

Rooted to the Land

Daryl realized in his mid-thirties that he didn't have a single hobby. It wasn't his fault; not really. For years his PhD program, part-time pastorate, and the ordinary requirements of family were all he could muster. Plus, we birthed three babies in five years. It's hard to get into mountain biking or fly fishing when you haven't had a proper REM cycle in months.

When we moved to our current house with its dust-patch backyard, he'd only just turned in his dissertation. We sat on plastic lawn chairs with In-N-Out Burger in our laps and surveyed the Venusian landscape. Dealing with the dirt patch was the last thing on my to-do list. I couldn't even remember which box had our spoons, and I'd been wearing the same pair of jeans for a week. But Daryl turned to me with a spark in his eye.

"We're going to grow things here," he said.

"Cool," I said. "Have at it."

Half a decade later, the landscape has been transformed. Our friend Jeff helped us select, plant, and stake a gingko tree (male, not female, because apparently gingko trees come in male and female, and the females spend half the year smelling like dog vomit? Good. To. Know). Michelle brought us boxes of succulent babies seeded from her garden. Daryl planted yellow zinnias and purple morning glories and pink sweet peas and lavender hollyhocks. He ordered a white nectarine tree and a yellow one, and then a clementine tree small enough to begin its life in a pot on the patio. He repaired sprinkler lines and purchased seed starters. He got sunburned and then slathered himself with SPF 50 and got sunburned again, until he finally bought the world's most hideous-and-yet-effective sun hat.

> **Land doesn't respond well to hurry. In that way, tending gardens and souls and children have a lot in common.**

Turning the backyard from a dust bowl to a garden hasn't come quickly. *It's been a labor of love and time over years, and it's still a work in progress.* Wendell Berry—and nearly every farmer ever—has noted that land doesn't respond well to hurry. In that way, tending gardens and souls and children have a lot in common, and Daryl now wakes most mornings and heads straight out to the yard to see what's grown, what's been nibbled on by a pest and needs attention, and what would benefit from more pruning or watering or a stronger stake.

"Ooh!" he exclaimed last night, looking at his phone.

"Bruins football?" I asked. Usually his chirps of delight have their origin in a good coaching decision.

"Organic cilantro seeds! On sale!"

He is not the man I married sixteen years ago, but gosh, I love watching this new side of Daryl emerge. The land is shaping him, even as he shapes the land. In *The Unsettling of America*, Wendell Berry writes, "[T]he care of the earth is our most ancient and most worthy and, after all, our most pleasing responsibility."[41] Even in our small patch of backyard, we've found this to be true. Knowing our place is shaping not only our backyard but our souls as well.

Committing to Care

A chapel speaker at my alma mater once cautioned us against choosing to marry someone "to make us happy."

"If you want to be happy, get a golden retriever," he said. "Marriage is hard work. Check that: Don't even get a golden retriever, because pet ownership is hard work. Get yourself a nice statue, or a rock."

Daryl and I go eight rounds every year on whether or not we should get a pet cat. I'm Team Cat, because I see all the delight one could bring to our family. He's Team Never Cat, because he knows a cat also means a stinky litter box and annual vet bills. He also gently reminds me that the indoor plants are my responsibility and that they are all currently dead. All organic things require care. It's true of cut flowers, carrots in the crisper, even the compost bin.

> As we work, the work also works on and in and through us, strengthening weak wills, teaching hard patience to hurried hands, opening eyes to awe and wonder.

I'll be honest—I want all the purrs and cuddles and none of the carpet clean-up. It's not dissimilar to parenting, where I burst with love and pride watching my children learn and grow and discover the world—but I'm desperate to be spared the mountain of laundry, the yearly bout with the stomach bug, and the never-ending quest for sleep.

The thing about living creatures is that they require something of us. And the thing about the love God calls us to learn and live—the love Paul writes of in 1 Corinthians 13, the love Jesus shows for us on the cross, the love of the Spirit pulsing over the dark waters before the world's creation—is that it seeks not just to fulfill requirements but to care lavishly, abundantly, beautifully, particularly. As Makoto Fujimura puts it in his exquisite book *Art & Faith*, "The God of the Bible is the God of abundance ... Love demands more than utility; a greater love expands purposefully into an expansive and enduring realm of relational depth ... God's purposefulness is not aligned with our notion of day-to-day pragmatic purpose."[42] Real love delights in the happiness of enjoying the beloved, but never treats the beloved—whether that is a person or a place—as the means to an end of selfish consuming.

We can read the mundane work of tending the land or the children or the soul as a product of the fall—bringing forth goodness only by the sweat of our brows and the blisters on our hands and the irritation tickling our minds. And surely this is one element at play. The work of loving another can be overwhelming or even crushing at times—too much for a person to bear. No one enjoys digging postholes in the blazing sun.

But there is also a gift and grace in elements of ordinary work and creation care, an opportunity to love well in the dailyness of life. The soil offers us lessons in this, as does the slow, stubborn, sacred growth of crops and marriages and friendships and children. As we work, the work also works on and in and through us, strengthening weak wills, teaching hard patience to hurried hands, opening eyes to awe and wonder.

These are lessons we simply cannot learn while on the move. And our transience can stunt more than just us. Like an abandoning parent misses their children's milestones but also wounds them by his or her absence, so uprooting too often can leave a path of devastation. Our home's backyard was a dust bowl when we moved in because its previous owners had a five-point plan to redo the landscaping. The plan began as follows: Step One—Kill all the grass. So they did. And then they moved away.

Storied Places

In her book *Native*, Kaitlin Curtice writes about rediscovering and reinvesting in her Potawatomi heritage, particularly the ways her ancestors valued the land. "The earth is always speaking," she writes, "but over time, we lose the ability to listen. If we are lucky, we return again. If we make room inside of ourselves for childlikeness, we will make room for the ability to learn again, to be small, humble people who ask questions instead of making demands, who listen to the land instead of carving it into pieces for profit. This is the way of being Indigenous."[43]

White Christians in particular have much to learn from our Native brothers and sisters—as well as our other brothers and sisters of color—about what it means to belong to the land rather than exploit it. They have rich heritages and profound wisdom, including their own stories within our sacred Scriptures. In her book *Abuelita Faith*, Kat Armas writes, "If we are to regain this sabiduría, wisdom, we must reclaim and reconstruct our spirituality, built on the backs of those who came before us, especially those who were overlooked or silenced."[44] The question is, Will we finally listen?

Part of committing to a place is committing to care for the land that's entrusted to us, however small a patch it may be. Whether a backyard or a window box, a plot in a community garden or acres upon acres of woodlands, one of the blessings of stability is the opportunity to tend with tenderness the land on which we reside. To do that, we will have to be open to the wisdom of those who have come before, who knew and respected the rhythms of season and weather. We may also need to reckon with the truth that the land on which we reside is not—and never will be—ours. It may have been stolen from Native people, like the land upon which I sit today, where the Acjachemen people resided until Spanish conquistadors decimated their numbers.[45] Today, fewer than two thousand of them remain.[46]

Creaturely Knowledge

When we first moved to Southern California nearly a decade ago, I felt like I'd been dropped in the middle of a Dr. Seuss book. Though I occasionally stumbled upon a familiar plant or animal—squirrels are pretty much just squirrels, apparently—the majority of the flora and fauna astonished me. The tree in front of our condo dropped giant, lacquered leaves that smelled like Vicks VapoRub. (Eucalyptus?) Huge red and yellow and pink flowers bloomed year-round. (Hibiscus?) Our first week in town I dropped a quarter under the community mailbox and, when I stooped to pick it up, discovered a spiky spider's egg sac straight out of a horror novel. (Brown widow! *shudder*).

> Part of committing to a place is committing to care for the land that's entrusted to us, however small a patch it may be.

I did my nerd thing and checked out half a dozen library books on local plants, but I returned them soon after the amount of biodiversity completely blew my mind. In the Northwoods of Wisconsin I could name nearly all the plants and animals, in part because I grew up homeschooled in a forest, and that was kind of our thing, but also because the species were fairly limited. Red pine, white pine, hemlock, and balsam would get you 90 percent of the way home with evergreens. Maple, oak, birch, and poplar covered the bulk of the deciduous trees. My library book told me there were six starter species of eucalyptus tree alone, and none were even originally native to California. Don't even get me going on cacti (dozens), succulents (hundreds), or native grasses (maybe ten trillion is a slight exaggeration, but only *slight*).

Frustrated with all I'd yet to learn to begin even scratching the surface of California's plant and animal life, I was tempted to give up entirely.

"It's a grey bird," I'd tell Lincoln when he asked. "A big tree. A purple flower."

Then I remembered the wisdom of St. Anne (Lamott) about overwhelming projects—we don't need to do everything at once. We can take them bird by bird. I didn't have to have encyclopedic knowledge overnight. Instead I could observe, ask questions, take in wisdom, and do it all at my own pace.

I started with a single tree outside our condo.

A red gum tree, as it turns out.

And so it began.

The Vultures

Dear neighborhood friends of ours moved away early one December, packing up their belongings, stacking moving boxes in the garage, gifting my kids little odds and ends they couldn't take with them. We grieved for weeks before they left, and we're still grieving, though they've now been gone for years.

The week before they loaded their van and left for Iowa, a giant flock of vultures flew into our neighborhood and perched in the tree above their home.

"Well, that's ominous," said Daryl. The kids—our three and their six—watched the birds with binoculars, marveling at their ruddy necks, their stooped posture, their giant wings. When we weren't watching them on purpose, we were often startled into looking up at them anyway because they are just so loud. They don't talk much, but they are heavy fliers, launching themselves from tree branches with a sound like a thousand shuffling decks of cards. We counted twenty-eight of them, and we watched each morning as they left the neighborhood soon after dawn. They'd return around six each evening. My mom called it "coming home from work."

A group of vultures is known as a committee if they're sitting in a tree: a fact that tickles me to no end, as a Presbyterian who has sat through more than my share of long, unnecessary meetings. On the ground—where they usually sit only to pick at a carcass—they're called a *wake*. Watching the vultures gave us something to chat about besides the gut-wrenching truth that our bonds of friendship were on the cusp of being altered forever. Of course, we promised to visit; we had every intention of keeping in touch. We haven't done the former, not yet; and we've dabbled in the latter; but no amount of email and FaceTime can compete with life lived across the street from one another, with unscheduled evening play in the cul-de-sac six nights a week. There is a simple grace in nearness that isn't easily replicated, despite all our technological advancements. Anyone who couldn't hug a niece or nephew or grandchild due to pandemic precautions or the expense of travel, instead watching them grow from afar, knows this profound ache.

The neighbors are well settled in Iowa now, tending orchards and attending Mass, but the vultures are still here with us, still coming home for the day around six, still hunching on their branches for the night, still spreading their wings anew every morning. The kids watch them, stilled for a moment from their bike riding. Daryl and I watch them, stilled for a moment from the dinner or the dishes or the trash cans that need to go out to the curb.

"A group in a tree is called a committee," I tell Daryl again.

"That's cool," he says, even though we both know I've told him this fact ten, twenty times. I repeat things like this. Stories, jokes, phrases. Being married to me is a little bit like signing on to lifelong sitcom reruns, which, luckily, Daryl also really enjoys.

Before the vultures, I never really noticed our neighborhood birds. I never noticed birds at all. When I was young, my mom would exclaim about the bald eagles fishing in the lake, and I'd yawn. My grandma would beckon me to the window to watch the ruby-throated hummingbirds she fed sugary water to, from a bright red plastic feeder, and I'd feign interest for a moment before quickly returning to my comic books. When Daryl and I moved our family to California, home of the famed swallows of Capistrano, I couldn't be bothered to pay any attention at all.

But then the vultures came, followed quickly by a pandemic that had us sitting at home for weeks, staring out the window and pondering our own mortality. Suddenly I began to notice a sweet little black-headed bird that sat on our fence and flicked its tail up and down. What species was it? A birding app taught me that it was a western phoebe, and the ones sitting on the peak of our roof were mourning doves. Over the next weeks we learned about our northern mockingbird, a pair of house finches, and three distinct varieties of gleaming, darting hummingbirds.

There is a simple grace in nearness that isn't easily replicated, despite all our technological advancements.

Creation burst forth in all its glory in our little backyard, strewn with children's detritus and newly broken sprinklers and crabgrass we'd decided to live with because sod is both expensive and reticent to grow in our desert climate. One bright-eyed, feathery body at a time, the birds began to save me, tethering me to our place, reminding me of the God who cared for them and would—even in this new, uncertain, plague-strewn landscape—care for each one of us, too.

My friend Paul is a bird-watcher and a physicist. We've never met in person, but his Twitter presence (the most appropriate social media site for a birder, I suppose) is a constant source of delight.

When he's down or work is difficult or life is just too life-y, he goes out into the woods near his home, stills himself, raises his gaze, and awaits, in his words, "a bird from the Lord." I've taken on Paul's practice as my own: birding as a spiritual discipline, quieting my body, standing still, looking up in holy expectation. The birds rarely disappoint.

Birds have little utilitarian purpose. They exist, at least in part, simply for our joy. They're the sunsets of the animal world, present whether we notice or not, but willing to lift our souls if we take the time to pause and watch. Yesterday I spotted a tiny goldfinch eyeing me from the scrubby undergrowth, its head cocked to the side, remaining still only a second or two before flitting from its branch into the deeper brush.

Remembering to pay attention can be the trickiest spiritual practice of all.

No one else was there to witness to it. I could have walked right by, except my shoe came untied. Slowly, ever so slowly, God is teaching me to look up, to look around, to slow down, to witness.

Remembering to pay attention can be the trickiest spiritual practice of all. Humans have always been terrible at keeping what's important at the forefront of our minds. In Deuteronomy, God tells the community of faith to literally tie the commands of God to their arms, to write them on their foreheads, to nail them to the doorposts of their homes: "Remember that you were slaves."[47]

It can be hard to see the ground right beneath our feet as holy. It's just plain old ground—carpet we're hoping to replace or tile we laid ourselves or a dirty sidewalk outside our office building or a path of earth packed down by the tramping feet of children. Yet God is at work right here, right now. Will we notice? Will we even remember to look?

California is a birder's paradise, and my repertoire quickly grew from the black-capped chickadees of my childhood—often the only songbirds hardy enough to stay the winter—to a dozen backyard species in regular rotation. An abundance of birds from the Lord, each one a tiny miracle of glossy feathers and bright eyes. There were lizards, too, big and medium and teeny tiny. We saw the occasional long-eared rabbit and a freaky possum that liked to scoot across the stone wall late at night, its pale face illuminated by the porch light like a hockey mask in a horror movie. One morning on a neighborhood walk, I was turned back by a patchy coyote, staring me down in cold calculation. (Not *all* fauna is benevolent.)

We started naming the animals that visited us or lived in our yard—Joe the crow, Larry the lizard, Phoebe the western phoebe (seemed appropriate). Aunt Jill taught us to dig sand crabs at the beach. Church friends showed us how to shuffle our feet while wading in the waves to alert stingrays to scoot away. Little by little we began to know our place in this new, fascinating locale. And with each creature we encountered, I felt my heart settle a little bit more into this place as home.

Questions for the Present

1

Are you good at remembering, or do you tend more toward forgetfulness? If you're forgetful, what do you forget the most often?

2

What do you love most about the geographical area where you live?

3

Who originally lived on the land where you reside? How might you learn more about the history of the people who were there before you? How might you honor their legacy?

4

Read Deuteronomy 5:15. How does God invite us to remember his goodness through the land?

5

What is one thing you want to learn about the land where you live? How can you pursue that knowledge this week?

CHAPTER 10

The Delight of Being Known

Love your crooked neighbor
with your crooked heart.

—W. H. Auden, "As I Walked Out One Evening"

ONE OF THE biggest barriers to joy is people. People like the Philistines who filled in Isaac's wells. People like that one neighbor who claims the best public parking spot on the street as his own personal property, sitting on his porch all day until he can snag it. People like that one lady at the PTA. People like the teenagers who shout the F-word at the playground, oblivious to (or worse yet, cognizant of) the toddler at your feet. Horrible, imperfect, difficult, unruly people. People like me. People like you.

It's an absolute fact that there will be friction anytime more than one person settles in a place. (Heck, there will be friction even when *only* one person settles there. Literature students know this conflict as "Man versus Nature," and it is its own type of difficulty.) Even within my own household—a man I adore so much I *married* him, children I birthed and fed from my own body—sometimes I want to run away and join the circus. Fostering community is some of the toughest, most painful work we can engage in. People are sinful bundles of trauma and unresolved issues. No wonder the local school board is such a mess.

Yet we are called to relationships for our own good, the good of the world, and the glory of God. God is so gung-ho about the importance of community that he sent his son, Jesus, to live among us, and the Holy Spirit to dwell within us. God himself—Father, Son, and Holy Spirit—*is* a community. One God, three Persons. If that blows your mind a little, welcome to the club. The Trinity is wiiiiiiild.

We are called to relationships for our own good, the good of the world, and the glory of God.

In theory, a community is a beautiful thing. In practice, a community is most often a very, very messy thing. It takes dedication, listening, patience, and conflict resolution. It is nearly—if not completely—impossible in the long term without divine help. It's good we serve a God who delights in drawing near.

● ● ●

Our church partners with a local Spanish immersion public school, seeking to help love and serve its students and teachers as Jesus would. Early in our tenure as pastors, when our babies were still tiny, we decided we would send our children there one day, too. Still, it was one thing to serve in mission occasionally, dropping by the school's community garden one Saturday a month or donating snacks to the PTA; it is another thing entirely to be at the school five days a week dropping off our own flesh and blood. We have literal skin in the game now. As the years go on, this school becomes more and more *our* school and its people *our* people—not as a project, but as a true community of friends and neighbors. God puts parents and classmates into our paths on a regular basis, and we form relationships simply by being present. By being us.

We planned to love and serve and give back out of a commitment to follow God's command to love our neighbors as ourselves. But—and isn't this a true missional cliché?—we've received so much more in return. Our oldest child is nearly fluent in Spanish; we've made friends from Mexico and Guatemala and Peru and right here in Orange County.

It has been good and right, but it hasn't always been easy. Folks we respect deeply have questioned our decision, asking if we'd seen the school's test scores (we had) and were sacrificing our children on the altar of mission work (um, no, but thanks for asking). The school often falls short of needed resources, scrambling for simple things like copier paper or hand sanitizer. My own grasp of Spanish remains terrible, barring me from communicating well with some of the parents in the pick-up line. This community blesses and stretches us—our family, our church. The blessing feels wonderful. The stretching can ache. Both are of God.

Who We Are

In an age of influencers and personalities, platform and celebrity, adventure and possibility, bigger and farther and larger and more are almost exclusively trumpeted as better. Yet the work of God is always particular and local. Jesus speaks of mustard seeds, of single coins. My denomination teaches that the elements used in the Lord's Supper must be "common to the local community," leaving room for the worldwide church to feast at the Lord's Table on loaves familiar to them, made from grains harvested nearby. Paul writes differently to the Philippians (*Good job and thank you!*) than he does to the Galatians (*Oh my word, people, stahhhp it!*). God spoke differently to and through Amos, the goat-herding prophet, than he did to and through Paul, the learned scholar.

Truth is unchanging, but translation is adaptive to time and place and culture. (I'll always love the story of Hans Egede, missionary to Greenland, who realized the Inuit people had no concept of or word for *bread*. So he translated the Lord's Prayer, "Give us this day our daily seal."[48]) God chose different metaphors in the psalmists' poetry than in the story of creation. The story of Jesus is universal, but our participation in it is very, very particular. We live out our faith right where we are, in ordinary days like today. It's the only way.

This is why knowing and being known—right here, in this place and time—is so essential. It is within the stability of a community and the grace of limits that we can learn to translate the gospel to our neighbors. How are they hungry for God? Where do they hurt? What do they long for? It is also here that we may find ourselves unable to run or hide, but instead known for who we are over the long haul and loved for who we are, too.

● ● ●

I've often believed that a life in motion is the highest good. Why settle down when you could keep on truckin'? Parenthood was one big shock to the system, as I found myself tethered to the house for nap time and mealtime and nap time again. Nearly every parent-to-be holds the ideal of continuing on in life as it was before children, going to the concerts or the breweries or the late-night-worship sessions and simply bringing the kids along for the ride. Before having children, I had not yet felt the crushing weight of endless sleepless nights or looked into the confused, distant, frantic eyes of a baby so fried with tiredness that he can't help but shriek with the pain of it. Marriage already changed everything; I don't know why I clung to the illusion that welcoming children wouldn't be at least as seismic a shift.

> The story of Jesus is universal, but our participation in it is very, very particular.

The Benedictines have a tradition of staying put that author Micha Boyett found particularly heartening in her early days of motherhood. She writes, "Benedict asked his brothers to 'make prayer the first step in anything worthwhile that [we] attempt.' If a day at home raising my son is not worthwhile, what else could be? I write this down ... I want to remember."[49] The constraints of place—sometimes to my very own home, because it was nap time for the littles *again*—are their own kind of difficult gift.

As a writer, it can be tricky to walk the line between craft and platform. Often the pressure to develop a big enough following for national sway is overwhelming. Books are a business, after all, and authors who can draw a crowd in both Cleveland and Carson City (not to mention on social media!) sell more books. Yet the pressure to create "content" rather than tending the soil of craft can make for an anemic voice.

Big can be beautiful, but local is decidedly intimate and transformative in a way big can never be.

As I've struggled through this balance in my own journey as a writer, I was deeply heartened by author Laura Lundgren's words on shifting her perspective to see herself not as a ladder climber with hopes of stardom but instead as a writer to her particular community: "[A]s a village poet, my ministry remains profoundly local. As a pastor's wife and a mom, the majority of my life takes place offline. Learning to see myself as a village poet has helped me to see my writing as a service to my neighbors rather than a pathway to personal fame."[50]

Laura's commitment to loving her neighbors inspires me. It helped me shift my own focus from BIGGER and BETTER and MORE to crafting sermons and custom Bible studies for my particular congregation, writing to a people I know and love deeply, with spiritual practices tailored to their specific needs in a given season. These sermons and studies are received by tens or hundreds, never thousands. But I get to see their impact and pray their prayers alongside my people. Big can be beautiful, but local is decidedly intimate and transformative in a way big can never be.

Seen and Known

Before Felicity's birth, a local friend asked if she could throw me a shower. I hesitated.

"Oh, that's right," she said, not missing a beat. "I remember now. You hate parties and small talk. I'm so sorry! No shower. How about you and I and a couple of friends go out to dinner together and get you a few gifts? Our treat?"

The joy of knowing and being known can deepen the more time we spend with people whom we love and who love us. Conflict will come—it is a mortal lock when dealing with humans—but as we learn to press in rather than run away, there is incredible joy ahead.

● ● ●

Don't get me wrong: It's scary, too. Being known takes vulnerability that can be difficult to muster. Early in our dating relationship I'd sometimes stop in the middle of a story, frustrating Daryl to no end. He finally pressed me on this awkward habit.

"I just don't want you to get bored with me," I told him.

He took my face gently in his hands and said, "Courtney, I could spend every minute of every day with you and you would still remain an infinite mystery to me. Boredom isn't even in the realm of possibility." (See why I married him, even though he opens tortilla chip bags like a grizzly bear?)

> **God invites us into relationships where we can be seen and known, loved and grown, first with him and then with our neighbors.**

Whether our fear is running out of stories to tell or sharing parts of ourselves that are less than glamorous, God invites us into relationships where we can be seen and known, loved and grown, first with him and then with our neighbors. And when we enter relationships of trust, greater knowledge will beget greater love.

And we could all use a little more of that.

Questions for the Present

(1)

Describe a time you felt really known by someone.
How did it feel?

(2)

What fears do you have about being known?

(3)

How does God invite us into greater vulnerability with
him? With trusted friends and neighbors?

(4)

Read 1 Corinthians 13:1–13. How does love lead us
to greater knowledge of God? Of ourselves?

(5)

How might you seek to know God more fully?
Yourself? Your neighbor? How might you invite God
and a neighbor to know you more fully?

CHAPTER 11

The Pleasure of Stillness

I live in tranquility and trembling.

—Annie Dillard, *Pilgrim at Tinker Creek*

THE HOUSE IS quiet this morning. The kids are at school, Daryl is at church, and I am alone at the kitchen table with only the calls of the birds from the yard and the hum of the refrigerator. Except, those sounds aren't my only companions. The Spirit is here, too. Pulsing, breathing, rushing, whispering.

I hear a crow, a song sparrow, and what I suppose is a mockingbird, though it's difficult to tell with mockingbirds. I hear a car start up across the street—Ben heading to work, the last month before his wife Negin will bear their child. I hear a mourning dove.

I hear from God.

It rained last night, the first thunderstorm we've had in over a year, and the birds are euphoric. Water brings life, insects and mice and the sprouts of dormant seeds from the hard-baked clay soil. The turkey vultures in the tree across the street would lick their lips in anticipation, if they had any lips to lick.

It's right to be suspicious of those who say they hear from God. News stories frequently quote deceivers or the deceived who cite God's voice as the reason they committed acts of unspeakable horror. Beyond the obvious pitfalls, there are the people who live their entire lives in neutral, waiting for a clear word from God that never comes.

> It is not our stillness that seats God upon the throne. It is our stillness that helps us refocus our gaze to the throne where God has been present all along.

"How would I know?" we ask. "There is so much noise."

In Scripture, even the resurrected Christ moves about largely unrecognized. Mary thinks he is the gardener. Cleopas walks miles alongside him but doesn't notice it's Jesus until they've reclined together at the table. If those physically closest to Jesus couldn't see him for who he was, what hope have I in distinguishing God's voice from all the sounds swirling around my Californian kitchen table in this twenty-first century?

"Here on the mountain I have spoken to you clearly," Aslan tells Jill in *The Silver Chair*. "Here on the mountain, the air is clear and your mind is clear; as you drop down into Narnia the air will thicken. Take great care that it does not confuse your mind."[51]

I am still new at tuning my ears to hear the voice of the Almighty. The practice of listening prayer, of sitting silently in the presence of God and simply waiting, is often the last thing I want to do. But for the last several years I've sought to press into the discomfort of quiet, to still my body and cease my many, many words, and to breathe deeply and wait in silence for God.

When we still ourselves in God's presence, it isn't God we're waiting for. God is always present to us, available, beseeching, attentive. We are waiting for our own heartbeats to slow, for our anxious thoughts to settle like sand on the ocean floor so we can see clearly down through the newly crystalline waters and into the depths below.

God speaks through the psalmist, "Be still, and know that I am God."[52] It is not our stillness that seats God upon the throne. It is our stillness that helps us refocus our gaze to the throne where God has been present all along.

The companionable silence of deep friendship, of childlike trust, of the firm belief that, as St. Julian once wrote, "All manner of things will be well," does not come quickly or without struggle. So often I am impatient. I want easy and quick, a one-off Bible verse that will act like a gummy vitamin, giving me all of the benefits with none of the bitter kale. I want salvation without the humility, sanctification without the discipline. I want to be better—so much better—than I am, but I don't want to confess or repent or admit my mistakes. I want bright and shiny when half of the Old Testament is illustrated in sackcloth—burlap!—and ashes, and nearly all the rest is either war or wandering.

God allows me to spin my wheels, patient as a mother awaiting the end of a tantrum. When my energy is spent, when I've told God all the reasons I can't possibly sit still today—I am a Very Important Person™ after all, plus the house is a mess and the sermon unwritten, and oh, I need to order that birthday gift for my niece, and we're out of yogurt again and the sink is still drip, drip, dripping—I sit down for just a moment and take a breath and finally acquiesce.

This morning from my kitchen table I hear the birds beginning to quiet down in the yard. The refrigerator hums. And here, in this stillness, a quiet joy trickles into my heart as I listen and God listens.

God is forever present to us.

Can we be present in response?

Can I?

God on the Shore

In college I spent a summer guiding whitewater trips down the Wolf River in central Wisconsin. It's a small river, hardly even worth rafting if you're from anywhere with bigger, wilder rapids. I guided the trips for campers and their families, but many outfitters in the area will rent a raft to tourists with no training at all—*Sign this waiver! Okay, good luck!* Despite its tameness, for kids from Wisconsin and Illinois—known for forests and farmland rather than outdoor adrenaline activities—kayaking down the

Wolf River was more than enough for a little thrill. Every weekday morning that summer, I'd load up a trailer with kayaks and a van with campers, and we'd head out to the rapids together.

I loved the joyful adventure of those mornings, not to mention the authority of being the adult in charge at the tender age of twenty-one. Before the summer began, the camp's directors paid for me to attend a Wilderness First Responder course, where we learned to splint broken legs with canoe paddles and bandage sucking chest wounds with Gore-Tex. I learned how to recognize signs of hypothermia and dehydration and sunburn, the importance of wound care, and how to identify a hot spot on a heel before it turned into a painful blister. Then I took CPR classes and lifeguard training with the other team members in the freezing, pouring rain. Late spring in Wisconsin always gives a run for the money weatherwise. The powers that be cut short our final exam—strapping a partially submerged, giant adult man to a backboard to protect him from a potential spinal injury— because every lifeguard-to-be in that lake had turned blue.

God is forever present to us. Can we be present in response?

I was trained, equipped, and certified, complete with my new title—Adventure Team Director. On the upper stretches of the Wolf River, I felt confident and at ease, even on days I had a pack of unruly third graders, hyperactive fifth graders, or anxious parents in my care. As we unloaded at the river, I would don my yellow personal flotation device with its upper straps narrowed to free my arms for paddling, strap my orange rope throw-bag to my orange kayak, and announce the day's instructions to the group.

In the parking lot, we'd have campers sit atop their kayaks until they were familiar with how to steer them and—more importantly—how to exit them in the event of a capsize. We didn't use the kayaks you may have seen on television in the Olympics—the ones with a skirt that sits around a person's waist and snaps into the boat's center hole. Exiting a skirted kayak takes quite a bit of practice and can easily go wrong for a newbie, trapping them underwater in a submerged boat.

Instead, we used sit-on-top kayaks featuring two wide padded straps lengthwise on the boat's top. These straps would each rest over a knee of the paddler, giving them leverage and control of their boat while still leaving them free to swim away if it tipped over.

"Sharon will take the front!" I'd chirp, nudging another twentysomething from our staff to grab her boat. "Danny's got the middle! I'll be in the back." The team leader always took up the rear. On a river, you want your strongest paddler at the very end of the group where they can see the whole line of campers and catch up with anyone who might be in trouble. Paddling upstream is nearly—and sometimes actually—impossible.

Our river journey was often the first our campers had ever undertaken, and they'd pepper me with questions.

"If we don't like it, can we get off in the middle?"

Sure, but there's nowhere to go but forest, so you might want to stick it out until the end.

"Will we see a bear?"

Only if we're really lucky.

"What's that on your life vest? Is *that a knife?*"

Yes, it is a rescue knife. That way, if your boat tips and you get stuck in the straps, I can—

"CUT MY LEG OFF?"

No, honey, I could cut the kayak strap.

"Oh. Phew."

The summer days whiled away one after the other. We'd have sun; we'd have rain. The river would rise and fall. Sometimes we had very few rapids to speak of and it'd be more of a lazy river float, but most campers were happy just to be outside while enjoying the freedom from mosquitoes a trip in motion provided. By mid-summer I'd only needed to pull out the first aid kit once, for a man who tipped his boat onto a sharp rock and scraped up his shin.

Then it was time for Big Smokey Falls.

During the young camper and family trips, we stuck to the upper stretches of the river with its flat sections and Class 2 rapids that rippled and bubbled but were generally quite tame. But when high school camp began, the lazy river just wouldn't do. High schoolers crave excitement and adventure, and many of them signed up for camp just to take a raft over Big Smokey Falls, a twenty-foot cascade at the very end of the river's lower section.

The camp owned its own kayaks, but for the high school trips we rented rafts and helmets from an outfitter just south of town. The morning before our big adventure, a few other staffers, a camp director, and I drove out to scout the lower sections of the river. We'd had significant rain and the river was moving high and fast—great news for our high school campers. A low river would mean their rafts would get stuck on rocks and shoals, leading to a much slower, more frustrating trip. A fast river was great news.

The upper stretches of the river looked fine—rip-roaring, but free from downed trees and other water hazards. It was the middle stretch that worried me. Sullivan Falls.

"Is that a hole?" I asked, pointing to a troubling bulge amidst a particularly large rapid. In whitewater parlance, holes are areas of recycled water where, instead of flowing downstream, rapids churn upstream in a cycle. Holes can trap a boat in their currents, which is inconvenient but not often dangerous. The real trouble comes when either the next boat down the river crashes in on top of a stuck one, or—worse yet—when a boat flips over into a hole. Getting trapped atop cycling water while in your boat is annoying; getting trapped underwater can quickly turn deadly.

We watched the bubbling rapids for a moment before I made an executive decision: "We're going to close the beaches for the Big Smokey trip and put our lifeguards here on the shore with rope throw-bags." While our beach lifeguards didn't have the river training our whitewater team did, they'd be extra eyes and hands, able to stand atop the small cliffs overlooking the most intense stretches of the rapids to throw a rope to anyone who got trapped or stranded. We confirmed our plan and returned to camp.

On the morning of the trip, the dining hall was abuzz. Teenagers strutted and bragged; they looked bright-eyed with anticipation or wide-eyed with fear. Together we loaded up for the river, my team and I slinging our orange and yellow kayaks into the van trailer, the teens piling into the bus. Once we hit the shore, we donned life vests and helmets and launched raft after raft into the water. I waved to the members of my team as they headed out. After the last raft of high schoolers pushed in, I nodded to our head lifeguard, who hopped back in the van to drive his team to their vantage point on the bluffs above Sullivan Falls, rope bags in hand. Then I said a prayer, buckled my helmet, and slipped my own kayak into the river.

The upper stretches went beautifully. I could hear the teens whooping and hollering and watched as the leaders guided them around outcroppings of rock and toward the deeper, faster stretches of river. I'd been fretting about this trip for weeks, but now that it was underway, I felt the sun on my shoulders and smiled up at the sky. A blue-green dragonfly buzzed by my boat on its way to the opposite shore. Shaggy pines lined the river like sentries watching over us on our journey down the roiling river.

I marveled for a moment that I got to do *this*—be out in nature, bouncing down rapids all day—for Jesus. I've never done well with traditional women's ministries that tend toward tea and conversation or fancy brunches or craft nights. There's nothing wrong with any of those things; they just don't suit me. I wanted to be on the move. I felt alive when I could help my campers draw parallels between the beauty of their lived experience on the river and the love of the creator God for them. To this day, I take as many pastoral care meetings as I can while hiking. A windswept hillside or a burst of wildflowers or a sunset often speaks so much more loudly than anything I might say in my office. Even in my visits to our local assisted living homes, praying together near a window sure beats facing the wall.

In her book *Dimming the Day,* Jennifer Grant describes this phenomenon in this way: "Being outside—or even looking at photos and watching videos of natural beauty—soothes us, as does experiencing wonder and awe in our imaginations as we contemplate the natural world."[53] There are few things more beautiful than a river on a sunny summer day.

A windswept hillside or a burst of wildflowers or a sunset often speaks so much more loudly than anything I might say in my office.

But I quickly refocused; there was work to be done. My throat tightened a bit as we turned the corner toward the river's middle section, but I pulled into an eddy by the shore and watched as, one by one, my team in their kayaks and the teenagers in their rafts sailed through. I noticed a flash of orange up on the bluffs—the lifeguards with their buoys and rope bags. Three rafts to go. Then two. Then one.

I breathed a huge sigh of relief and offered a quick prayer of thanksgiving. There were bigger rapids farther down the river—

including Big Smokey Falls, which always gave the teens a huge thrill—but nothing as potentially troublesome as this hole. I pushed off into the river for my turn.

As I lined up my boat for Sullivan Falls, I suddenly felt that something was off. Maybe I didn't push off far enough into the river; perhaps I just hit the current at a funny angle. Time moved in slow motion as I scrambled to adjust my center of gravity and paddled frantically, desperate to avoid landing in the hole. I glanced up at the bluffs, ready to yell for the lifeguards to spot me.

No one was there.

They'd left.

My heart leapt to my throat, I went over the falls, and my kayak turned over.

The next moments were a blur of terror and whitewater and desperation. I popped free from the boat, which sailed downstream without me while I tumbled over and over in a cycle of churning rapids that kept pushing me back upstream and underwater. I grabbed a breath in each fraction of a second it spit me to the surface before plunging me down again. I hadn't enough air or time to scream for help. With the lifeguards gone and my team around the bend of the river, no one would have had the time to reach me anyway.

My friend Amanda is an experienced kayaker, and just the week before she'd told me a story of a friend who'd escaped a hole by unbuckling his life vest.

"Isn't that a *bad* idea?" I'd asked.

"Sometimes if you get stuck in one of those churning currents, you can't get out on top," she told me. "You have to sink down and swim out underneath."

As the edges of my vision began to grow dark, I reached for the buckle on my life vest, ready to kick down into the river's dark and icy depths. As I felt it click, the river suddenly relented, spitting me downstream to flat water, where I gasped and heaved and burst into tears. The rest of the rafts having turned the corner, no one had noticed me fall in. I wiped my eyes, rebuckled my vest, and swam to my boat, which was now stuck in a patch of reeds by the opposite shore.

"You can fall apart later," I told myself. "Right now, there are high schoolers out on this river, and you're in charge."

I did indeed fall apart later, after we'd driven back to camp, stowed the kayaks, and sent the campers off to dinner.

"That sounds so scary," my friend said as I sobbed in her arms. "Near-drowning is a serious thing."

It took me a few years to process the depths of my moments alone on the river, but as I have, I've learned that it wasn't even the near-drowning that scared me the most. It was that I was completely alone. I don't fault the lifeguards—they did their job up until the next-to-last moment, and after watching dozens of teens make it through successfully, they never expected me to be the one who fell into trouble. I could have been clearer with them about their role, about the importance of staying put until everyone made it through; that's on me. But I will never forget looking up to that bluff for reassurance, for a reminder that someone had my back in this moment of crisis, and realizing there was no one there to save me.

A God of Presence

There have been seasons in my life where God has felt as absent as that lifeguard on the cliff. Just when I need the Almighty, I look, and there's only emptiness.

The psalmist cries out words of abandonment: "My God, my God, why have you forsaken me?"[54] Jesus echoes them while he hangs on the cross.[55] Throughout history, from prison cells and concentration camps, refugee settlements and welfare offices, hospital rooms and cemeteries, suffering people cry out to God: *Where were you when I really needed you? I looked up to the bluff in my distress, and you had abandoned me.*

Sure, it's lovely to share a joy with God. He has an open invitation to all of my celebrations, and I often sense his presence in the flickering birthday candles or the hearty feast. But we can bear joy pretty well on our own, when push comes to shove. It's in those moments of darkness and terror, uncertainty and fear, pain and torment that we need assurance of God's presence the most.

It wasn't even the near-drowning that scared me the most. It was that I was completely alone.

And yet, sometimes, these are the moments we sense him the least.

In that river, I'd had a powerful sense of God's love and presence on the upper stretches. I didn't feel him at Sullivan Falls. I felt only alarm and dread. I wasn't just abandoned by the lifeguards; God seemed absent as well. Diana Butler Bass writes of a near-drowning experience at age three when she got pulled into deep water by a wave at the beach. She writes, "As I rolled beneath the waters, my eyes opened and I saw the sun, bright but oddly indistinct at the same time, its light diffused all around me, drawing me toward its source."[56] Her impressions were of timelessness and beauty. Mine were not.

We are never left alone, even when we don't sense God's presence.

I was fine in the end, of course. As an outside observer, I see God's hand in releasing me from that hole despite the lack of lifeguard support. I see God's hand in having me be the one in distress rather than a fourteen-year-old, or even one of my teammates. I would have volunteered to be the one to struggle rather than have any of them experience what I did. I see God's hand in my kayak stuck in the reeds, waiting for me.

I finished the trip. Heck, I finished the summer (though I will admit I volunteered for many more shifts at the rock-climbing wall than the river after that). Before long I was headed to seminary to serve the same God whose presence I could not feel in that river.

Because here's the thing: Feelings are only part of that story.

Praise God for that, because in any given day my feelings can make wild swings based on nothing more than the weather and how much caffeine I've ingested. It isn't that our feelings don't matter—they matter profoundly—it's that they cannot be allowed to drive the bus.

Our kids love this book series by Mo Willems about a naughty pigeon. This pigeon wants all sorts of things—hot dogs, cookies, but most of all, to drive the bus. The bus driver tells the readers *not* to let the pigeon drive the bus, and then the driver leaves, so of course the pigeon spends many, many pages trying to convince children to allow him this honor. You can't let a pigeon drive a bus, though. The pigeon can *ride* on the bus, of course. But it can't be allowed to drive.

Seasons of Change

The majority of us will go through seasons like Jesus and the psalmist, searching in vain for God's voice when he seems utterly silent. I have no answers for why this is so. I do, however, cling to the dual lessons from them both—first, that we are never left alone, even when we don't sense God's presence. Secondly, the story is a long one, and the valley of the shadow is never the final word. Christ's anguish from the cross is followed by resurrection. The psalmist's tortured cry resolves in hope.

The more I stop running from the darker depths of my feelings toward God, whether they be abandonment or anger or—one of the scariest for me—anxiety over what feels like divine aloofness—the more I find God's presence even amid the pain.

Questions for the Present

1

When have you felt closest to God? Farthest away?

2

Have you ever felt completely abandoned by God? When was it and what was it like?

3

Read Psalm 22:1–11. What permission does this psalm offer for you to bring the depths of your emotions to God?

4

What is the significance of Jesus quoting from this Psalm while on the cross?

5

Read Psalm 22:22–24. How does the resolution to this psalm's anguish strike you? Where is God when we feel such anguish?

CHAPTER 12

Good Trouble

Community is always a risk.

—Jonathan Wilson-Hartgrove, *The Wisdom of Stability*

I KNOW YOU'RE in there, Bill!"[57] I shouted, standing on the frosty front lawn of a quaint, Victorian-style home. "I'm here because we love you."

I wasn't professing romantic intentions; rather, I was trying to coax a recalcitrant congregant out of his home. He'd stormed off after a meeting—one I'd thought had gone well—and I had no idea why. After days of calling (with no answer) and a week of emailing (ditto), I finally just put my boots and coat on and walked over. After all, he only lived a block from my house. That's the thing about small-town ministry: You can run, but not far. And there's nowhere to hide.

Bill finally opened his front door, standing there with a smile.

"Pastor!" he said. "How nice to see you."

So, this was how he was going to play it.

"Good to see you too, Bill," I said. "Do you have a minute to chat?"

"Not really. See, I was just heading out to—"

"He has a minute," his wife appeared behind him, shoving him gently out the front door. "He definitely has a minute."

Bill and I walked back behind the house to his garage, where he showed me his latest project—repairing the engine of an aging truck. We talked about his grown kids. We talked about his dogs as they frolicked and tussled under our feet. And then I broached the question that dangled between us like a piñata just waiting to be given a good whack with a broom.

"So … about that meeting?" A flush of red began to creep up his neck.

"She knows what she did," he said, his features hardening into a scowl.

"Who?" I asked.

"Julie!" he exclaimed, incredulous. Out poured a story of decades of feeling slighted by a woman in the church who had more influence, more money, and more power around town. Tales of being ignored, passed over, disparaged. I listened to his pain: the pain of a proud, soft-spoken man who'd scratched out a life for himself in a hardscrabble farm town where many families went back six generations or more. I stood respectfully until he finished. Then we prayed together, and his shoulders squared.

"Thanks," he said. "I didn't know all that was in there."

"Thank you for trusting me," I said. "Now, how can we work together in all of this? We want to listen to you. I want to listen to you. Your voice is just as important as anyone else's in that room. But we can't hear what you don't say."

"That's fair," he said. "Maybe next time I can try to speak up."

"I'd love to help," I said. He broke into a chuckle.

"I can't believe you just stood on my lawn and yelled. How long were you going to stay there?"

"I blocked out the afternoon," I said.

"That's a long time."

"I'm pretty stubborn."

"So am I," he said.

"I know. That's why I blocked out the afternoon." We both began to giggle.

● ● ●

I stood in Bill's yard because I've had friends stand in mine. Not literally, but in many other ways and times and places. Being present to a loved one means we do the work to meet them where they are, however we can. Of course, there are times we need to let people go—when the cause really is lost, or the person simply does not want to accept a relationship with us, or we need to erect strong boundaries for the sake of our families or our children or our souls. But in every relationship—even healthy ones—there will be seasons of difficulty to navigate where we have to stand in a metaphorical yard and yell, "I love you!" to see if anyone will come outside. We may even have to block out the afternoon.

In seminary, I spent entire years with my head down just trying to get through the day—three part-time jobs, Hebrew homework, cockroaches in our decrepit apartment, Daryl living two thousand miles away in Nashville to start his PhD—yet my friend Katie simply wouldn't let me disappear.

"Knock, knock!" she'd yell from outside my door.

"You don't have to say that," I'd yell back. "You can just knock."

"I have smoothies!" she'd yell.

"I have homework!" I'd yell back. This is around the time our next-door neighbor would start pounding on the dividing wall, and I'd remember she had a new baby and I should stop yelling. I'd crack the door, and Katie would bound into the room.

"Katie, I don't have time for—"

"You have to eat, and you've been alone all week, and friends show up when you need them."

"But I don't—"

"Yeah, you do. Here, have a smoothie. Strawberry banana." Katie saved me that season with her smoothies and her yelling. Bill and I saved each other, talking through his years of pain and conflict and helping him return to those church meetings with his voice strengthened and renewed. Jesus doesn't break down the door; he stands and knocks. But he's persistent, too. Wherever we are, he is there.

Detours Galore

The musical *Come from Away* describes the tiny Newfoundland town of Gander on the day of September 11, 2001. As the US government struggled to make sense of the day's unfolding tragedies, it shut down national airspace, forcing airplanes already en route to divert to other countries. Thousands of passengers landed in Gander, the closest North American airport to most flights inbound from Europe. Disoriented and afraid, they disembarked on Canadian soil, uncertain of what would happen next.

In the song "Wherever We Are," the guests fret about the dark forests and patchy information. In "Welcome to the Rock," the chorus sings of the rugged beauties and idiosyncrasies of Gander—its rough weather, its isolation, its people who have persevered through everything from abominable winters to local characters. The passengers on those planes never planned to visit Newfoundland, and yet, there they were. It was time to adapt, to reorient themselves, and to make the best of sleeping on a church pew or a Lions Club carpet. The town rallied, ensuring every passenger was fed, clothed, and housed, even throwing a party when it became clear the passengers would be staying more than a couple of days and everyone needed a joyful diversion.

Jesus doesn't break down the door; he stands and knocks.

"If you want to make God laugh," the old saying goes, "tell him your plans." Few of us end up exactly as and where we imagine. Every passenger on an airplane on 9/11 saw their plans disrupted. Our days are much the same—perhaps not often in ways as big as being rerouted to Newfoundland, but filled with detours just the same. In college, I studied to be a journalist and then an English professor, only allowing God to turn my heart to ordained ministry after years of prayer and struggle because *surely* women couldn't do that—could they? Should they? Should *I*? California was never on my list of places to live until God—and Daryl—put it there. We were certain our family was complete with two children, but now we couldn't imagine our household without Felicity's sparkle and spunk.

Detours come at us in small ways, too. The flat tire, the expired milk, the package we're waiting for that doesn't show up when we need it, the raaaaaaaaaaain on our wedding day. Practicing the presence of God wakes us up to the hand of God in these fits and starts of our lives. Instead of needing perfectly placed plans, our eyes become attuned to the wind of the Holy Spirit that blows where it will.

Our former children's ministry director once shared the story with me of driving down the central road in our city and hearing God tell her to turn the car around.

"So what did you do?" I asked.

"I turned around, of course," she said. And just a few blocks down the road in the new direction, she saw someone in need of her help.

In his book *Joining Jesus on His Mission*, author Greg Finke describes our work not as being on mission for God but in coming alongside God where the work has already begun. It's a subtle but deeply important shift: the difference between me incorrectly assuming I'm bringing God to a situation and properly understanding that God is always already at work. As Fleming Rutledge puts it in her book *Advent,* "God is on the move toward us, not the other way round. In the very midst of our confusion and incapacity, we are met by the oncoming Lord."[58]

I often speak to people nearly immobilized by their fear that they will miss what God wants them to do. My answer is always the same: "Keep your eyes open. God isn't in the business of hiding." While we can—and do!—obfuscate and ignore, when our goal is obedience, God will make the way plain. This is not to say the way will be simple or easy or without challenge. We will often feel trepidation, anxiety, and even fear when undertaking a new challenge, accepting a life-changing call, or rooting out an old sin. Yet God is always the first actor, and the goal of the Almighty is never to cause chaos or confusion but instead to bring order, blessing, and new life. The first signs of unsettledness that often begin when God is at work are simply a troubling of the waters—God stirring our souls to help us remember to look up and around, to be aware so we are ready for what will come next.

Small Trouble

We owe a lot to the family who lived in our house right before us. They cared for the aging air conditioner and kept an eye on the plumbing and maintained the rose bushes out by the road. But the thing I'm perhaps most grateful for is their fight for the neighborhood crosswalk.

A quarter mile or so from our house is a sweet little park with a soccer field and a hill, some big pine trees and a playground. At sunset people sit on blankets and watch the colors spread over the houses below. On the weekends the soccer field is always filled—sometimes with children, other times with sweaty adults. To get to the park, many of us need to cross a fairly busy street at the top of a hill. Visibility for drivers is poor, and there's no stop sign. You see the problem.

> **The goal of the Almighty is never to cause chaos or confusion but instead to bring order, blessing, and new life.**

When we first moved in, I'd put all of the kids into a wagon and pulled them across as fast as I could. It didn't matter if I looked both ways, because cars roared around the corner and up the hill in a flash, often leaving me scrambling to get to the sidewalk before disaster struck. Lincoln, nearly five years old when we moved in, was deeply bothered by having to ride in the wagon *like a baby*. I held my ground, bolstered by visions of broken legs or worse.

Then, a few months into our tenure, I pulled our blue wagon around the corner to see a new yellow sign and freshly painted white stripes across the road. A crosswalk. We had a crosswalk! The cars slowed. The kids cheered. I even allowed Lincoln to walk across on his own. It was a new day in our little neighborhood for anyone heading to the playground.

"I guess the city finally realized what a hazard that crossing was," I told Daryl over dinner.

"Oh no, it wasn't that," he said. "It was Mrs. Fritz." He went on to tell me how the previous owner fought for years. She wrote letters to the city and then went around the neighborhood gathering signatures for a petition. "She fought for a safer crossing, and then they moved away before they ever saw it happen." The kinship I'd always felt in my heart for the family who sold us their beloved home so we could make it ours blossomed anew.

"Thanks, Mrs. Fritz!" chirped Lincoln. "Next time I'm gonna *ride my bike* across the street!"

Taking on the Task

The longer we are present in a place, the more its problems will begin to be ours, too. We will rejoice with those who rejoice—the neighbor who lands a new job, the friend who welcomes a new baby, the local school that wins an award—but we will also weep with those who weep. In that weeping, if we listen closely, we may also hear God calling us into action. In her book *Glorious Weakness*, Alia Joy writes, "We are hardwired for self-deception and self-preservation, but the Word of God is intrusive. Disruptive. Subversive."[59] The closer we draw to the God of love, the harder it will be to close off our hearts and ears to the cries of those in need.

● ● ●

Father Greg Boyle is something of a Los Angeles legend. Boyle was ordained as a Jesuit Catholic priest in 1986 in East Los Angeles. His first church assignment was in the Boyle Heights neighborhood, an area rife with gang violence. Boyle quickly found his heart rent by the suffering and bloodshed. Something had to be done. By 1988 Boyle had helped found an alternative school and daycare program, and from there, a bakery, which proved so successful Boyle was able to found Homeboy Ministries, "America's largest gang-rehabilitation centre."[60] Much of Boyle's good results came from walking alongside people as holistic beings, not just violent problems to be solved. Homeboy Ministries—and its sister programs, Homegirl Café and Homegirl Silkscreen and Embroidery—offer employment training, but also counseling services, tattoo removal, educational classes, and legal help.

Boyle describes the story in his book *Tattoos on the Heart: The Power of Boundless Compassion.* The book is not a celebration of Boyd's ministry success, but rather a reminder of our common humanity and God's call to something far richer and more beautiful than we often settle for. Writes Boyle, "This book ... does aspire to broaden the parameters of our kinship. It hopes not only to put a human face on the gang member, but to recognize our own wounds in the broken lives and daunting struggles of the men and women in these parables."[61] The first step in beginning to truly love our neighbors as ourselves is simply to see them, and to see ourselves in them. When this happens, they become not an "other," but the beloved of God.

So do we.

Treading Gently—and Firmly

We've learned at our church that it is all too easy to rile a congregation when talking politics. Buzzwords carry weight; voting records signal loyalty or disloyalty to this group or that. So, we don't talk politics. But we preach the whole of Scripture—which is robustly political, even if all you do is read the prophets and the Gospels and take them seriously. And we talk a whole lot about loving people.

Here's what I mean: If you asked ten of our congregants their views on immigration, you'd likely get nine and a half different answers. But when we asked them if we should collectively sponsor an Afghan refugee family, the support was nearly overwhelming. Likewise, their concern and care for teachers, students, and families at Viejo Elementary—our local Spanish immersion school—is deep and consistent. The same has been true for the ways our congregation has rallied to bless the marines at Camp Pendleton just down the road.

We cannot cede God's command to love our neighbors to our favorite political party.

There are politics, and then there are people. Partisan politics quickly cause division, but they do perhaps their greatest harm by lifting us from the particular to the universal, swapping tangible care for a neighbor for an impersonal program. Don't get me wrong: Many, *many* systemic injustices and problems need systemic fixes in addition to local ones. But we cannot cede God's command to love our neighbors to our favorite political party (or even the one that simply makes us the least nauseous). The work is ours, too. And ultimately, it is God's.

You may not be called to work for an end to gang violence. Then again, you probably don't live in East Los Angeles, either. But maybe there's a crosswalk needed on your street, or a new neighbor struggling to learn English, or a company exploiting its workers, or a wetland about to be bulldozed. Listen closely. Who is weeping? Where might God be inviting you to step into the fray, for the good of the kingdom?

Let's get into some good trouble.

Questions for the Present

1

What is a small problem in your area that needs fixing? A bigger one?

2

Have you ever been part of a solution to a local problem?

3

Read James 1:26–27. Who are the "widows and orphans" (i.e., people on the margins who may need extra love and care) in your community?

4

How does focusing on local community (church, school, neighborhood, etc.) help us move from partisanship to the common good?

5

How might God be calling you to invest in some good trouble where you live?

CHAPTER 13

Be All Here

What world is this I now inhabit,
and how shall I live in it?

—Kate DiCamillo, *The Beatryce Prophecy*

Early on in our dating relationship, Daryl and I often struggled to connect over the phone.

"Dial it in, Court," he'd say. "I feel like you're only half there."

"Oh," I'd tell him, "my housemates just came home, and I didn't want to be rude and leave the room. We haven't seen each other in days." He'd sigh.

"I'd rather have ten focused minutes with focused you than an hour with distracted you."

I'm a master multitasker. You don't pastor a church while raising small children without being one. I'm on the phone with the pediatrician while feeding one child a snack and giving another a thumbs-up as he walks the backyard slackline. I schedule piano lessons for our oldest while our youngest is napping and our middle building his afternoon blanket fort so I can send a couple of quick emails. I regularly cook dinner while helping with homework, refereeing whose turn it is to play with the train set, and responding to comments from my editor.

There is a joy to this frenetic season of life, with its perpetual motion and never-ending To-Do lists. There is also a price to be paid for my near-constant distraction, as I realized just today when the birthday gift I purchased online for my sister arrived on my own front steps. Oops.

Daryl is a quality-time guy, and even today, with so many years of marriage under our belts and no secrets between us, what he wants most is my undivided attention, leaning in, listening, fully present to him. After a day of keeping all the church-and-family plates spinning, it can be hard for me to settle in to this deeper, quieter way of being. Yet this is where the bonds of our relationship are strengthened, as I give the fullness of myself over to the fullness of who he is. Even ten minutes of chatting about our days, both of us connected to one another, makes an outsized difference in our marriage. Being present to another person tells them of their value to us and our love for them. And these moments will also strengthen our love, because the moments of being fully present help us to know more deeply, which in turn grows our love.

● ● ●

Two of my very best friends live thousands of miles away from me. We keep up mostly on a video chat app, our busy lives and schedules running on different time zones. I leave one of them a message. A day or so later she leaves me one in response. Yet in seasons of serious straits—one's appendicitis, another's adoption, my own midlife crisis tattoo—we respond to one another differently. It isn't enough to leave a video to be watched later; we'll also text and remind the friend we are right there, present and available no matter the time of day or night.

> Being present to another person tells them of their value to us and our love for them.

True friendship is leaving your ringer on when you're a sleep-deprived parent of young kids. Seriously though.

There is a kinship that forms when we give our full selves to another person, our attention, our time, our focus, our presence.

To Remember

After taking his sabbatical at a Benedictine monastery in Italy, Jackson Clelland, our church's senior pastor, returned home with a newly discovered deep love for fixed-hour prayer. Jackson is our staff adrenaline junkie—at home on steep mountain bike trails, motorcycles, and surfboards—so his nascent commitment to a scheduled prayer life surprised me.

"It frames the day," he said. "It reminds me that it all begins and ends with God."

Though no one on our staff has yet adopted the monastic habit of regularly rising before dawn for prayer, many of us have been encouraged to set timers or put aside particular windows in our days—waking, meals, the moments before drifting off to sleep—for regular prayer. Even a moment or two, when given frequently, adds up to a good amount of time. Plus, those consistent pauses are powerful when it comes to remembering God's presence with us.

We are such forgetful people. Much of our dedication to presence must simply begin with remembering: God is present; God is listening; God is love; God is good.

Digital devices are a deadly poison when it comes to practicing God's presence. In a moment of lag or boredom or mental space, we now hold the possibility for near-infinite distraction in the palms of our hands. What if we could train ourselves to connect first to the Creator of the universe before pulling that phone from our purse or pocket? Worlds would change, and not because of our own self-control, but because we would begin to remember with greater regularity how loved we are and how deeply the world longs to be reminded of this, too. Fixed-hour prayer is one way to stave off the madding crowds of the internet, if only for a few moments at a time.

> We cannot spend our lives running from pain, nor can we avoid it any other way. It takes courage to remain present even so.

The Pain of Presence

One of the things that holds us back from being fully present, fully alive, is that when we are in touch with all of our nerve endings, we will almost certainly experience greater pain than when we go about our days in a state of metaphorical sleepwalking.

Numbing behaviors usually arise for a reason—we've been hurt in the past, or we've tried unsuccessfully to make a change, or the situation of our life or work is too exhausting or overwhelming or fraught with boredom to face straight-on.

"When we lose our innocence," writes Annie Dillard, "when we start feeling the weight of the atmosphere and learn that there's death in the pot—we take leave of our sense. Only children can hear the song of the male house mouse. Only children keep their eyes open."[62]

It makes absolute logical sense that the more pain we experience, the more we pull inward. And as the man in black tells Buttercup in *The Princess Bride*, "Life *is* pain, highness. Anyone who says otherwise is selling something."

We cannot spend our lives running from pain, nor can we avoid it any other way. It takes courage to remain present even so. We will often not succeed. But we can return to it time and again, sowing habits of stillness, watchfulness, kindness, humility, and love.

It is the only way.

Today I watch my children grow up in Southern California, their hair bleached nearly white by the sun. They are growing into beach kids—great swimmers, unafraid of the crashing waves, drawn into deeper waters with their boogie boards and fins.

I still don't feel fully at home in Orange County. I will (forever, I fear) miss some of the social cues; I forget my sunscreen; I keep waiting to be sent back to my childhood habitat of snowy forests. After eight years, when people ask me where I'm from, I'm just beginning to end my answer in a different way:

"I grew up in Wisconsin and studied in Chicago, New Jersey, and Nashville. But California is my home."

Questions for the Present

1

When do you feel most at home? Least?

2

What is one thing that you love to do that helps you connect to the people and place where you live?

3

What spiritual practices help tether you to your current people and place?

4

Have you ever considered practicing fixed-hour prayer? Why or why not?

5

How might God be inviting you to connect more deeply to your place and people through spiritual practices? What is one you might try this week?

CHAPTER 14

Standing Amazed

The wilderness remains the same,
but we are changed.
And because we are changed,
the wilderness is transformed, too.

—Alicia Akins, *Invitations to Abundance*

ALMOST EVERY exhausted, frazzled parent of young children has had a run-in with a person who says, "Treasure every moment." I've had this phrase lobbed at me during the middle of my three-year-old's meltdown at Target; while holding a squirming, squalling, sick baby at a doctor's office; and as I purchased the fourth pair of sneakers in a single school year for my rapidly growing preteen. I always want to snap, "No, I will not! Some moments are not worth treasuring!"

The comment comes from a good, nostalgic place, I'm sure, but it's not often helpful. We parents of young kids feel guilty enough already. We *know* we are on our phones too much. We *know* this time is fleeting and precious. We *know* that we will miss these sweet, simple days when nearly all of our children's immediate problems can be solved with a Band-Aid or a Popsicle. But also, we are tired. We are so very, incredibly, ridiculously tired. We haven't had a REM cycle in days or a really restful night's sleep in a decade. We are so tired we find our hairbrush in the refrigerator and just shrug because, yeah, that happens. Just this morning Lincoln came bounding into our bedroom, excited to get ready for school before the light of dawn because he's in third grade and *third grade is awesome*, and I was so tired I rolled over and told him to just grab the car keys and drive himself.

Maybe it isn't about treasuring, but instead seeking to be present to the moment we are experiencing.

"Mom, I'm nine," he said.

"You're tall for your age," I said. "Just stick to side streets."

I wish there was a way for us parents to bottle an hour of our children's lives at every age and stage so we could revisit it when we weren't so darned crispy. What would it be like to nuzzle my infant's downy head after a full night of sleep and far from the throes of gnarly postpartum recovery? How delightful would it be to enjoy each of my children during their toddler phase, on a sunny afternoon when I am an octogenarian longing for time with tinies? But alas, time is linear, and this moment is all I have. Tomorrow my children will be older, and next week they will be older still. Someday I will sleep through the night and be oh, so grateful for it, but the wispy curls of our middle child will have straightened, and the baby will be borrowing my shoes while the oldest is away at college. I weep at the thought of it, but also, we have to keep moving along, because this current stage is unsustainable.

Perhaps *treasuring* isn't the right instruction. Not every moment is for cherishing. I would be happy to forget some of the exploding diapers, stomach viruses, and 4:30 a.m. wake-up calls that have marked our early days of parenting. Not all moments are enjoyable, and treasuring the rotten ones seems ill-advised. Maybe it isn't about treasuring, but instead seeking to be present to the moment we are experiencing. The more present we are to the gift of being all in, right where we are, the more we will discover the amazement of the incredible, exhausting, bright, beautiful, messy world God has set before us.

In Light of Eternity

We seek to be present because each moment is a gift, and also because we are not sure how many more moments lie before us. The fourth president of Wheaton College, V. Raymond Edman, gave a chapel talk to the students in 1967. He spoke about living in the presence of the King and then, midway through, suffered a fatal heart attack. He went from speaking about eternity to experiencing it in the blink of an eye. I think about President Edman when I get up to preach. Is what I'm saying true and beautiful and right and good enough that I'd be ready to say it before a heavenly audience? It's a good reminder that the heavenly audience is present every time I preach, even if I haven't yet met my creator face-to-face.

The early church spoke often about the end of life; so often, in fact, that they had a Latin phrase they often used: *Memento mori*—remember you will die. The first American churches often dug graveyards right outside the doors, making it hard to escape the knowledge that your time on this earth was short and soon you'd join your ancestors in the ground. Reminders of eternity change how we live now. They help us acknowledge our humanity and our frailty: that we are like "the grass of the field," as Scripture tells us, "which is here today and tomorrow is thrown into the fire."[63] It is in this transient reality that we find the joy of the Lord. Joy because we have this moment, right here, right now, today. This moment contains infinite possibility and opportunity and grace and light, but we will miss it all if we are not paying attention.

"This is the day that the LORD has made," the psalmist reminds us. "Let us rejoice and be glad in it."[64] This day, today, is a gift from God. There will never be another just like it. This is the only one we are guaranteed.

Some days, just getting through the day is gift enough.

Other days, a single moment can transform the rest of our lives.

Either way, being present makes a profound difference in how we experience the gift.

Present for the Present

My friend Alicia lives in Washington, DC, and often says the most difficult part is how transient the population is. It's difficult to put down roots if everyone around you is on their way to somewhere else. I've heard similar stories from friends in New York City, as well as from pastors who minister in college towns. If we love deeply, our hearts are broken on the regular by those who move away after only a short time. If we pull back and refuse to get attached, our lives suffer from a poverty of relationships. Do we choose the pain of loss or the pain of isolation? Why isn't there a third possible path marked by painlessness?

This day, today, is a gift from God. There will never be another just like it. This is the only one we are guaranteed.

No matter our circumstances, it is impossible to walk a pain-free path. Relationship involves risk. Being present takes work. Loving deeply will inevitably mean losing deeply. My great-grandmother lived to be 103 years old, and I can only imagine what it may have felt like to see friend after friend die. Gram lost her husband fairly early in life due to a freak accident at his workplace; she would eventually bury two of her own children; she slowly listened as the sounds of her downtown Chicago neighborhood—roving groups of children playing under the streetlights and immigrant families chatting on porches late into the evenings—transformed from these noises into the silence of older, gentrified professionals.

She lost much by loving deeply, but she would have lost even more by not loving at all. It is in the gifts of relationships, presence, conversation, and community that our lives are birthed and formed. We can stay safe and apart, but our spiritual deficits will only increase. To love is to experience loss, but the greater loss comes in never having loved at all.

Alicia knows this, continually recommitting to her church and her neighborhood despite the comings and goings of so many. She herself will go eventually—she knows that—but rather than pull in and away, she continually gives of herself, hosting meals for her housemates, serving her church as a deacon, connecting with her neighbors. Alicia espouses the wisdom of good old Willie Nelson: Wherever you are, be there.

Beach Vibes

Daryl's dad is on the time-share board of a condo complex at a beach town half an hour south of us. Once a year or so he offers us a week of free vacation, to which we say a resounding yes and thank you. We pack up boogie boards and wet suits and enough food to cook dinners in the little kitchen, and we take our annual minitrek. The first few years we did this, I found myself lost in the effort of keeping a family going at a new location. As a headline from *The Onion* once quipped, "Mom Spends Beach Vacation Assuming All Household Duties in Closer Proximity to Ocean."[65]

> To love is to experience loss, but the greater loss comes in never having loved at all.

"It's me," I said, texting the article to Daryl.

We just got back from this year's trip, and I went with a single goal this year: to be present. Present to my kids, to Daryl, to myself. Present to Jesus in the quiet moments that stretched out after the kids went to bed, and in the hour I'd steal after lunch to go for a walk up and down the hilly sidewalks. Present to my emotions. Present to the glory of the landscape. Present to the gift of vacation.

I didn't succeed completely or fail entirely. I am learning. It is a journey. But as I strove to cultivate new awareness, amazement rose to the surface like cream in my coffee, drifting up through the murky depths to bloom upon and brighten the surface.

At night I'd crack open the sliding door to the porch to listen to the pounding surf. *Amazement.* In the mornings I'd stand by the window and take a deep breath at the sunrise. *Amazement.* At night I'd sit in the living room with my kids and their stacks of library books and infinite art supplies and just watch their faces: the furrowed brow of the nine-year-old, the eye for detail of the five-year-old, the intense concentration of the three-year-old. *Amazement.* After we tucked them in bed for the night, Daryl and I would sprawl together on the sofa and talk and remember and laugh and cry. *Amazement.*

Nine years ago, we traveled to this same California condo for the very first time. We boarded a plane in the midst of a Wisconsin winter deep freeze, and the first morning I felt the Orange County sun on my skin, I sat on the beach and wept. Our oldest son was only a few months old; Daryl was deep in a PhD program; and I had worked my way into intense overfunctioning at my dear church. The frost hit early that year, and we felt frozen inside and out. Something needed to shift. I felt the sunlight on my skin and prayed a prayer of desperation.

Dear God, I implored. *Please help us figure this out. We are so tired. We need your help.* Over dinner one night we dreamed about me going part-time in order to spend time with my baby and write my first book. We dreamed about the end of Daryl's PhD graduation. We dreamed about making a life in California, closer to his family and childhood friends. We dreamed about the ease of living in a temperate climate while raising kids. We dreamed, and we worked, and we prayed. *Amazement.*

I'm not allowed to quote any Mary Oliver (poetry permissions are weird), but she writes a great deal about amazement, and there's a poem about being married to it that you should absolutely read. Go ahead, I'll wait. David Wright, another perennial favorite of mine, wrote about how his students would often choose the easiest research paper topic instead of one that would trouble them, but that those who chose a thorny, tricky, sticky topic often became transformed. He likens the difficult topic to a tulip bulb, swallowed by a student:

> *Staining our papers, our desks, our fingers*
> *Forever. And we would never get the smell from*
>   *our nostrils.*
> *The aftertaste would sting like liquor on our tongues.*[66]

Hardened or Broken Open

Many of the people I know who have lived through great trauma are either incredibly present or incredibly absent. Those who have pressed in and through the pain have a new empathy and awareness. Those who have ignored or shoved it down often live from distraction to distraction, never fully engaged with the moment in front of them. I am not judging those for whom this is true—there is a point at which we all break rather than bend, and not all harm is repairable in this life. Yet it is this first group I want to focus in on—those who have walked the valley of the shadow and come out the other side engaged and amazed and able to be present in a deepened way.

My dear friend Anna suffered a difficult season of infertility and then pregnancy loss. At one point, a ruptured ectopic pregnancy nearly ended her life. Years after this trauma, after a long season of praying, soul-searching, and adoption applications, she and her husband, David, welcomed an infant girl by adoption at the height of the pandemic. Their community rallied with support and meals and virtual baby showers to welcome little Jarena, and the depth of Anna's joy was profound.

During one late-night conversation she mentioned to me that being an adoptive parent was a kind of delight she hadn't anticipated. "When Jarena reaches for me, it still surprises me even after the six months we've spent together," she said. "I expected a baby to love me if that baby came out of me, but Jarena and I have no biological connection. Yet I am fully her mom. It's a deeper kind of joy." Anna then stepped back her words, not wanting to hurt my feelings since I am a biological mom of three.

"I am not offended in the least!" I said. "I can see how there would be a unique joy to the bond you and Jarena have. It isn't as assumed or expected. It might be a little bit like the joy of Daryl asking to marry me. He didn't *have* to." In the Christian story, we are taught that the bonds of baptism are deeper and richer than even the bonds of blood. Our kinship with Jesus isn't about our family or our ethnicity or our connections or even our good behavior. It's about being grafted into the family of God, to use another vineyard metaphor. In fact, Paul's favorite illustration for the community of Christ in Scripture isn't a family; it's a body. Each part different and valuable, unique and important, with Jesus as the head. No one is left out because they are single or widowed or childless or from the wrong side of town or a bloodline marked by scandal.

Many of the people I know who have lived through great trauma are either incredibly present or incredibly absent.

I love the metaphor of a body because the differences inherent in the distinct parts—ears and eyes, arms and legs, spine and sinew—are part of their strength. While we may have been told there was a particular way to be a good daughter or son, the right way to be a sister or brother, the proper way to be a mother or father, the strength in a foot is that it is simply that. As Paul writes, "Now if the foot should say, 'Because I am not a hand, I do not belong to the body,' it would not for that reason stop being part of the body."[67] I've heard dozens of stories from single friends of how painful it can be when the church focuses on traditional, nuclear families as the default unit for ministry. Not only is it uncaring toward those who are single—or single again, through widowhood or divorce—but it weakens the body of Christ by leaning too heavily on one particular body part at the expense of all the others. The same is true when we skew our focus too heavily on a certain age group or put white, blond baby Jesus in the manger.

Our church is working to see all its members—as well as its larger community—and not simply relying on patterns of the past that tended to assume a certain family structure. This is not to say that families don't need care, attention, and support— they certainly do! But so do the singles. The same likely holds true in your experience—there is a unique joy in friendship with people who are very similar to you in age or life experience or passion (just check out a tailgate party in Green Bay, Wisconsin). And there are other joys—and tremendous opportunity for learning—to be found when you connect with people outside those narrow categories.

There are blessings I've experienced—carrying and birthing and nursing—that Anna likely never will. But unless we end up adopting down the line, there are blessings she is experiencing that I will never know firsthand. I love that she shares them so freely with me.

Amazement.

Waking Up

Our second church service Sunday mornings is called the Awake service. I can't take any credit for that; a team formed it years before Daryl and I arrived. The tagline is "Opening our eyes to God's purposes." Here is the gift of being present in the present to the present: It is only here that we encounter the presence of the Lord.

In his Advent devotional, Walter Brueggemann writes,

> The whole tenor of Advent is that God may act in us,
> through us, beyond us, more than we imagined, because
> newness is on its way among us.... Advent is not the
> kind of 'preparation' that involves shopping and parties
> and cards. Such illusions of abundance disguise the true
> cravings of our weary souls. Advent is preparation for the
> demands of newness that will break the tired patterns of
> fear in our lives.[68]

So often we sleepwalk through life, our noses pressed to the
grindstone, our eyes tuned not "to sing God's praise," as the
old hymn goes, but to make sure we get to the dentist on time
and change the oil and deal with that squeaky doorknob. God is in
the business of bursting through our busyness with absolute
gobsmacking glory.

I am tasked not with moving the needle at all but instead with witnessing the inbreaking of the kingdom. I don't *do*; I merely tell the story.

The shepherds in their fields did not expect it. The wise men at their divinations did not expect it. Mary did not. Joseph did not. We do not. And yet there it is, time and time again: *amazement*.

Back when I was still starry-eyed about ministry, I met a
Lutheran minister and exclaimed about what a wonderful
profession he served.

"You must love making such a difference!" I gushed.

"You never make as much difference as you hope," he responded. I have chewed over his words for two decades now, and at times they've brought me solace, and at others, despair. Why serve the church if I'll never move the needle closer to love and truth and beauty and justice? But also it's a comfort to know that even this minister, whom I respect deeply to this day, was not able to move that needle much.

The older I get, the more I realize how true it is that the work, ultimately and completely, is the Lord's. We can participate and join in; we are invited to partake and jump aboard. But all the best-laid plans of mice and men (and ministers!) pale in comparison to the divine story unfolding before us.

The longer I serve in ministry, the more I realize I am tasked not with moving the needle at all but instead with witnessing the inbreaking of the kingdom. I don't *do*; I merely tell the story. I don't make the news; I report it. I don't draft the blueprint; I pour the concrete where the Great Contractor tells me it should go. I am a servant always, only, and ever. So are we all.

And herein lies the amazement.

Questions for the Present

1

Read Psalm 23. What speaks to you
in this passage today?

2

Read Psalm 23 again, but this time replace any
imagery with local imagery. For example, if you don't
live near green pastures, maybe replace it with a local
park, or your backyard, or the desert landscape in
your community. How does connecting this psalm to
your local place change your reading of it?

3

Read Psalm 23 a final time, focusing on God's
presence with and within you, right where you are.

Acknowledgments

EVERY BOOK is the product of a community. Without mine—church, neighborhood, friends, family—this book never would have come to fruition. To all those who have lived and are living life alongside me, thank you.

To all the good folks at Tyndale House and Hendrickson/Rose Publishing, I'm so grateful to each and every one of you. Thank you to Lynnette Pennings, managing editor extraordinaire; to John Ribeiro, Paul Hendrickson, Cristalle Kishi, Libby Dykstra, Anisa Baker, and the entire team. Deep thanks to Kay ben-Avraham, editor of insight, whimsy, and the best side-note comments ever.

To Bob Hostetler and the Steve Laube Agency, for their ongoing wisdom, kindness, and expertise.

To Jackson Clelland, senior pastor with a heart of gold, thank you for doing the work alongside Daryl and me to be here together. Same team always.

To Frank and Karen Allen for the tour of Bearing Fruit Vineyards and all their generosity and wisdom (and tractor driving lessons!).

To Aaron J. Smith for recommending Scrivener (bless you).

To Paul Wallace for the birding joy.

To Michelle Montjoy and Kevin Grump for tacos and backyard chats and reminders that good art can help save the world.

To Jill Ellis and Judd Westover for the lessons of sand crabs, boogie boarding, hospitality, and good wine.

To Del Belcher, who will never stop trying to get me on TikTok. It ain't happening, but I love you for trying. Thanks for being both a cousin and a friend.

To Alicia Akins for being a voice of gentle, prophetic wisdom. To Inga Wildermuth for sticking with me across continents and decades. To Steven Harsono for late-night puzzle chats. To Sonia Justl Ellis for being the voice of whimsy who helps me remember my soul. To Anna Woofenden for pastoring me as a friend and befriending me as a pastor.

To my writerly friends, for working at the craft, making the world a better place, and seeking truth and beauty: Aarik Danielsen, April Fiet, Stephen Kamm, John Graeber, Collin Huber, Kelsey Hency, Paul Pastor, Bethany Rydmark, Lyndsey Medford, Moriah Conant, Jodi Collins, K. J. Ramsey, Holly Oxhandler, Marlena Graves, Molly Jasinski, Karen Swallow Prior, Heather Thompson Day, Katelyn Beaty, Catherine McNiel, Michelle Van Loon, Micha Boyett, Kate Boyd, Shawn Smucker, and Susie Finkbeiner, and so many more—thank you, one and all.

To my pastor friends, for helping teach me the deep faithfulness of staying put for as long as God invites and allows: Carol, Steve, Bill, Jaime, David, Eileen, Elizabeth, Kathy, Cathy, Tom, Ross, John, Jon, Kay, Karen, Ephram, and Kevin.

Acknowledgments

To our neighbors on the cul-de-sac. Community in theory is nothing; community in the flesh is everything. Thank you for being our people! I'm so glad we can have block parties again.

To my church, beloved friends all, too many to name by name. You know who you are.

To my Belcher and Ellis families, with love.

To Lincoln, Wilson, and Felicity, the joys of my heart.

And to Daryl, always and always and always forever.

Bibliography

"Acjachemen History." *Juaneño Band of Mission Indians, Acjachemen Nation. http://www.juaneno.com/history.html.*

"A Statistical Analysis of the Art on Convicts' Bodies." Posted December 24, 2016. *The Economist. https://www.economist.com/christmas-specials/2016/12/24/a-statistical-analysis-of-the-art-on-convicts-bodies.*

Akins, Alicia J. *Invitations to Abundance: How the Feasts of the Bible Nourish Us Today.* Eugene, Oregon: Harvest House, 2022.

Armas, Kat. *Abuelita Faith: What Women on the Margins Teach Us about Wisdom, Persistence, and Strength.* Grand Rapids, MI: Brazos Press, 2021.

Auden, W. H. "As I Walked Out One Evening." *Collected Poems.* Ed. by Edward Mendelson. New York: Vintage Books, 1991.

Augustine. *On Christian Doctrine* (Book 1). *New Advent. https://www.newadvent.org/fathers/12021.htm.*

Aymard, Eliane. "On C. S. Lewis and the Narnian Chronicles." Interview with Rev. Walter Hooper. *Caliban,* no. 5 (Janvier 1968): 137.

Barr, Heidi and Ellie Roscher. *12 Tiny Things: Simple Ways to Live a More Intentional Life.* Minneapolis: Broadleaf Books, 2021.

Bass, Diana Butler. *Grounded: Finding God in the World—A Spiritual Revolution.* New York: HarperOne, 2015.

Benner, David G. *The Gift of Being Yourself: The Sacred Call to Self-Discovery.* Downers Grove, IL: IVP Books, 2015.

Berry, Wendell. *The Unsettling of America: Culture & Agriculture.* San Francisco: Sierra Club Books, 1996.

Bonhoeffer, Dietrich. *Life Together: A Discussion of Christian Fellowship.* Trans. by John W. Doberstein. San Francisco: HarperSanFrancisco, 1978.

Boyett, Micha. *Found: A Story of Questions, Grace & Everyday Prayer.* Brentwood, TN: Worthy Publishing, 2014.

Boyle, Gregory. *Tattoos on the Heart: The Power of Boundless Compassion.* New York: Free Press, 2010.

Brazil, Ben. "After Several Delays, a Park Honoring the First People of Orange County Could Open This Summer." Posted July 1, 2021. *Daily Pilot. https://www.latimes.com/socal/daily-pilot/entertainment/story/2021-07-01/putuidem#:~:text=The%20sacred%20sites%20and%20lands,1%2C900%20members%20in%20the%20tribe.*

Brown, Brené. *Rising Strong: How the Ability to Reset Transforms the Way We Live, Love, Parent, and Lead.* New York: Random House, 2017.

Brueggemann, Walter. *Celebrating Abundance: Devotions for Advent.* Comp. by Richard Floyd. Louisville, KY: Westminster John Knox Press, 2017.

Byassee, Jason and Ross A. Lockhart. *Better than Brunch: Missional Churches in Cascadia.* Eugene, OR: Cascade Books, 2020.

Come from Away. 2021; script, music, and lyrics by Irene Sankoff and David Hein, dir. Christopher Ashley.

Curtice, Kaitlin B. *Native: Identity, Belonging, and Rediscovering God.* Grand Rapids, MI: Brazos Press, 2020.

DiCamillo, Kate. *The Beatryce Prophecy.* Illus. by Sophie Blackall. Somerville, MA: Candlewick Press, 2021.

Dillard, Annie. *Pilgrim at Tinker Creek.* New York: Harper Perennial Modern Classics, 2013.

Ellis, Daryl. Twitter. Posted September 4, 2021. *https://twitter.com/revdarylellis/status/1434263636202061826.*

Finke, Greg. *Joining Jesus on His Mission: How to Be an Everyday Missionary.* Elgin, IL: Tenth Power, 2014.

Fujimura, Makoto. *Art & Faith: A Theology of Making.* New Haven, CT: Yale University Press, 2020.

Gladwell, Malcolm. "Choice, Happiness and Spaghetti Sauce." February 2004. *TED. https://www.ted.com/talks/malcolm_gladwell_ choice_happiness_and_spaghetti_sauce?language=en.*

Grant, Jennifer. *Dimming the Day: Evening Meditations for Quiet Wonder.* Minneapolis: Broadleaf Books, 2021.

Joy, Alia. *Glorious Weakness: Discovering God in All We Lack.* Grand Rapids, MI: Baker Books, 2019.

Lansing, Alfred. *Endurance: Shackleton's Incredible Voyage.* New York: Basic Books, 2014.

Lewis, C. S. *The Silver Chair.* New York: Collier Books, 1970.

Lloyd-Jones, Sally. *The Jesus Storybook Bible: Every Story Whispers His Name.* Illus. by Jago. Grand Rapids, MI: Zonderkidz, 2007.

Lundgren, Laura. "Village Poet." Posted March 11, 2019. *Plugged In to the Vine. https://servantsofgrace.org/village-poet/.*

McKnight, Scot and Laura Barringer. *A Church Called Tov: Forming a Goodness Culture That Resists Abuses of Power and Promotes Healing.* Carol Stream, IL: Tyndale Momentum, 2020.

Merritt, Carol Howard. *Healing Spiritual Wounds: Reconnecting with a Loving God after Experiencing a Hurtful Church.* New York: HarperOne, 2017.

"Mom Spends Beach Vacation Assuming All Household Duties in Closer Proximity to Ocean." Posted August 9, 2013. *The Onion. https:// www.theonion.com/mom-spends-beach-vacation -assuming-all-household-duties-1819575406.*

Nicholls, David. *Us: A Novel.* New York: Harper, 2014.

Pastor, Paul J. *The Listening Day: Meditations on the Way*, vol. 2. Portland, OR: Zeal Books, 2017.

Peterson, Andrew. *Adorning the Dark: Thoughts on Community, Calling, and the Mystery of Making*. Nashville, TN: B&H Publishing, 2019.

Peterson, Eugene H. "The Good-for-Nothing Sabbath." Posted April 4, 1994. *Christianity Today*. *https://www.christianitytoday.com/ct/1994/april-4/good-for-nothing-sabbath.html*.

Prior, Karen Swallow. *On Reading Well: Finding the Good Life through Great Books*. Grand Rapids, MI: Brazos Press, 2018.

Ramsey, K. J. *The Lord Is My Courage: Stepping through the Shadows of Fear toward the Voice of Love*. Grand Rapids, MI: Zondervan Reflective, 2022.

Reiner, Rob, dir. *The Princess Bride*. 1987; Act III Communications, Buttercup Films Ltd., The Princess Bride Ltd.

Rohr, Richard. "The Scandal of the Particular." Posted March 19, 2018. *Center for Action and Contemplation*. *https://cac.org/the -scandal-of-the-particular-2018-03-19/*.

Rutledge, Fleming. *Advent: The Once & Future Coming of Jesus Christ*. Grand Rapids, MI: William B. Eerdmans, 2018.

———. Twitter. Posted September 4, 2021. *https://twitter.com/ flemingrut/status/1434193004286382084*.

Sorkin, Aaron, dir. *Being the Ricardos*. 2021; Culver City, CA: Amazon Studios and Escape Artists; New York: Big Indie Pictures.

Taylor, Barbara Brown. *An Altar in the World: A Geography of Faith*. New York: HarperOne, 2009.

Teresa of Avila. *The Interior Castle*. Trans. Mirabai Starr. New York: Riverhead Books, 2003.

Thurman, Howard. *The Mood of Christmas & Other Celebrations*. Richmond, IN: Friends United Press, 2011.

Tolkien, J. R. R. *The Return of the King.* New York: Ballantine Books, 1965.

Villodas, Rich. *The Deeply Formed Life: Five Transformative Values to Root Us in the Way of Jesus.* Colorado Springs: Waterbrook, 2020.

Vischer, Phil and Skye Jethani. "Episode 448: Beth Moore's Exit & the Problem of 'Impoverished Imaginations' with Karen Swallow Prior." Posted March 17, 2021. *The Holy Post Podcast. https://www .youtube.com/watch?v=HagNiWW-qAk.*

Ward, Benedicta, trans. *The Sayings of the Desert Fathers: The Alphabetical Collection.* Kalamazoo, MI: Cistercian, 1975.

Warren, Tish Harrison. *Liturgy of the Ordinary: Sacred Practices in Everyday Life.* Downers Grove, IL: IVP Books, 2016.

"Why Do We Sleep?" Posted July 1, 2015. *The Independent. https:// www.independent.co.uk/life-style/health-and-families/features/ why-do-we-sleep-10358539.html.*

Wikipedia, s.v. "Hans Egede." Last edited June 28, 2022. *https:// en.wikipedia.org/wiki/Hans_Egede.*

Wilson-Hartgrove, Jonathan. *The Wisdom of Stability: Rooting Faith in a Mobile Culture.* Brewster, MA: Paraclete Press, 2010.

Wright, David. "What I Wish You'd Heard," no. 58. *Lines from the Provinces.* CreateSpace, 2000.

Notes

Introduction: Wherever You Are

1   Jeremiah 31:5.
2   For situations of domestic abuse, call the National Domestic Violence hotline: 800-799-7233. For situations of church hurt, I highly recommend *A Church Called Tov,* by Scot McKnight and Laura Barringer; *The Lord Is My Courage,* by K. J. Ramsey; and *Healing Spiritual Wounds,* by Carol Howard Merritt.
3   Benedicta Ward, *The Sayings of the Desert Fathers*, 139.

Chapter 1: Death to Ferns

4   Isaiah 65:21–22.
5   Alfred Lansing, *Endurance*, 94.
6   Rich Villodas, *The Deeply Formed Life*, 41.
7   Revelation 21:1–7.
8   Sally Lloyd-Jones, *The Jesus Storybook Bible*, 220. It should be noted that this idea did not originate with her, but with J. R. R. Tolkien in *The Return of the King*, 283. Sam Gamgee greets a newly resurrected Gandalf with awe: "Gandalf! I thought you were dead! But then I thought I was dead myself. Is everything sad going to come untrue?" Many thanks to Kay ben-Avraham for Tolkiensplaining this one to me in the most winsome possible way.

Chapter 2: Drawn to the Well

9   Genesis 26:3.
10 Phil Vischer and Skye Jethani, "Episode 448: Beth Moore's Exit & the Problem of 'Impoverished Imaginations' with Karen Swallow Prior."
11 Acts 17:23–24.

Chapter 3: Building Houses

12 I'll take my royalty check now, please.
13 Jeremiah 29:4–7.
14 Tish Harrison Warren, *Liturgy of the Ordinary*, 80.

15   Jason Byassee and Ross A. Lockhart, *Better than Brunch*, 105–6.
16   Warren, *Liturgy of the Ordinary*, 124.

Chapter 4: Planting Vineyards
17   Name has been changed.

Chapter 5: Less Really Is More
18   Malcolm Gladwell, "Choice, Happiness and Spaghetti Sauce."
19   David G. Benner, *The Gift of Being Yourself*, 57.
20   2 Corinthians 12:9.

Chapter 6: The Miracle of Sabbath
21   Eliane Aymard, "On C. S. Lewis and the Narnian Chronicles."
22   "Why Do We Sleep?", *The Independent*.
23   Eugene Peterson, "The Good-for-Nothing Sabbath."
24   Paul J. Pastor, *The Listening Day,* vol. 2, 25.
25   Exodus 23:10–13.
26   Howard Thurman, *The Mood of Christmas & Other Celebrations*, 51.
27   Barbara Brown Taylor, *An Altar in the World*, 156.

Chapter 7: The Scandal of Particularity
28   Philippians 4:6 NLT.
29   Leviticus 19:18.
30   Augustine, *On Christian Doctrine*.
31   Psalm 24:1.
32   Daryl Ellis (@revdarylellis), Twitter, September 4, 2021.
33   Fleming Rutledge (@flemingrut), Twitter, September 4, 2021.
34   Richard Rohr, "The Scandal of the Particular."
35   Annie Dillard, *Pilgrim at Tinker Creek*, 81.
36   Dietrich Bonhoeffer, *Life Together*, 23.
37   Numbers 11:14–15.
38   1 Kings 19:3–7; Jonah 4:1–11.
39   Numbers 11:10.
40   Numbers 11:17.

Chapter 9: Know Your Place
41   Wendell Berry, *The Unsettling of America*, 14.
42   Makoto Fujimura, *Art & Faith*, 78.

43 Kaitlin Curtice, *Native*, 8.

44 Kat Armas, *Abuelita Faith*, 41.

45 "Acjachemen History." *Juaneño Band of Mission Indians, Acjachemen Nation.*

46 Ben Brazil, "After Several Delays, a Park Honoring the First People of Orange County Could Open This Summer."

47 Deuteronomy 6:4–9; 11:18–21; 5:15.

Chapter 10: The Delight of Being Known

48 Wikipedia, s.v. "Hans Egede."

49 Mica Boyett, *Found*, 23.

50 Laura Lundgren, "Village Poet."

Chapter 11: The Pleasure of Stillness

51 C. S. Lewis, *The Silver Chair*, 21.

52 Psalm 46:10.

53 Jennifer Grant, *Dimming the Day*, 11.

54 Psalm 22:1.

55 Matthew 27:46.

56 Diana Butler Bass, *Grounded*, 12.

Chapter 12: Good Trouble

57 Names have been changed.

58 Fleming Rutledge, *Advent*, 342.

59 Alia Joy, *Glorious Weakness*, 95.

60 "A Statistical Analysis of the Art on Convicts' Bodies," *The Economist*.

61 Greg Boyle, *Tattoos on the Heart*, xiv.

Chapter 13: Be All Here

62 Annie Dillard, *Pilgrim at Tinker Creek*, 91.

Chapter 14: Standing Amazed

63 Matthew 6:30.

64 Psalm 118:24 ESV.

65 "Mom Spends Beach Vacation Assuming All Household Duties in Closer Proximity to the Ocean," *The Onion*.

66 David Wright, "What I Wish You'd Heard."

67 1 Corinthians 12:15.

68 Walter Brueggemann, *Celebrating Abundance: Devotions for Advent*, 3–4.

OTHER BOOKS BY COURTNEY ELLIS

Happy Now: Let Playfulness Lift Your Load and Renew Your Spirit

Courtney Ellis recounts a courageous—and often hilarious!—experiment in joy and delight as she awakens to the truth that God doesn't just want us to be holy, but happy too! You'll discover there is almost nothing that playfulness cannot make a little bit better and easier—and a lot more fun.

ISBN: 9781628628944

Uncluttered: Free Your Space, Free Your Schedule, Free Your Soul

Courtney Ellis shares her journey from a life of stress, stuff, and burnout to the abundant life of peace, space, and fulfillment that God offers. You'll learn tips for paring down your possessions, simplifying your schedule, and practicing the ancient art of Sabbath.

ISBN: 9781628627916

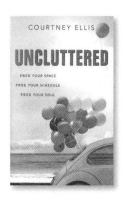

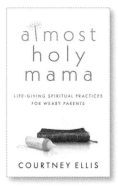

Almost Holy Mama: Life-Giving Spiritual Practices for Weary Parents

With the honesty of a close friend, the hilarity of a late-night comic, and the humility of a mom up to her eyeballs in diapers and dishes, Courtney Ellis invites you to draw closer to God amid the joyful, mundane, exhausting days of young parenthood.

ISBN: 9781628627909

Available at www.HendricksonRose.com